Hans Hasler

The

GOETHEANUM

A guided tour of the
building, its surroundings
and its history

Sophia Books

Sophia Books
Hillside House, The Square
Forest Row, RH18 5ES

www.rudolfsteinerpress.com

Published by Sophia Books 2010
An imprint of Rudolf Steiner Press

Originally published in German under the title *Das Goetheanum* by Verlag am Goetheanum, Dornach, in 2005. This revised edition of the authorized translation into English is published by kind permission of Verlag am Goetheanum

Translated from German by Christian von Arnim and Matthew Barton

A catalogue record for this book is available from the British Library

ISBN 978 1 85584 249 6

Interior design by Gabriela de Carvalho
Cover layout by Andrew Morgan Design
Printed and bound in Malta by Gutenberg Press Ltd.

Contents

Preface

With this guide I would like to introduce the reader to the Goetheanum building, its surroundings and its history – just as I would take an interested visitor on a guided tour. The first impression thus gained can then be deepened through subsequent encounters, attending events at the Goetheanum or by studying the extensive literature.

An encounter with the Goetheanum is as individual as each of its visitors. I first saw it at the age of fifteen from Blauen, through a pair of binoculars during a hike; this led me to want to become better acquainted with the place. Others hear or read about it, see pictures of it, or perhaps they happen "by chance" to take part in a guided tour of the building. Others again may have been familiar with anthroposophy for a long time and finally take the opportunity to see the place where key events in the history of the movement took place. Irrespective of any such previous acquaintance, this guide simply aims to provide some basic information for everyone.

Some of the texts draw on earlier work in this field. Information about these previous publications can be found in the bibliography. Warm thanks are also due to friends for their critical and very helpful comments and to Christian von Arnim and Matthew Barton for the wonderful translation into English and – very important – to the Anthroposophical Society in Switzerland which with a donation made this translation possible.

Hans Hasler

The Goetheanum and the School of Spiritual Science

An overview

The Goetheanum was first conceived as a building for anthroposophy. From 1909 onwards, Edouard Shuré's mystery plays and Rudolf Steiner's *Mystery Dramas* had been performed in rented theatres in Munich during annual conferences of the Theosophical Society (more on this in the chapter on the history of the Goetheanum). A building was to be constructed for these events whose external forms also expressed what lived within it. A visible expression of anthroposophy was to be created, not in concepts and ideas as is possible in books and lectures, but as living experience in artistic forms, in architecture, painting and sculpture.

The Goetheanum has many tasks today. To begin with, it is a building for theatre and eurythmy. The main auditorium, which can seat 1000, and the correspondingly large stage are used with several smaller spaces for rehearsals and performances by both the Goetheanum ensembles. The repertoire includes regular eurythmy performances as well as in-house theatre productions, but also guest performances and concerts. Major performances of Rudolf Steiner's *Mystery Dramas* and *Goethe's Faust* – performed here at full length and without any cuts in 1938 for the first time in theatrical history – deserve a special mention. Since that time Faust has been performed every few years in alternation with the *Mystery Dramas*.

Then the Goetheanum is the headquarters of the Anthroposophical Society. The Society is represented throughout the world and is structured in the form of groups or branches at a local level, national societies at a regional level and has its international centre here in Dornach in the form of the General Anthroposophical Society.

The heart of the society is formed by the School of Spiritual Science which is also based at the Goetheanum. Its task is to undertake research in the spiritual field, to provide stimulus for expanding and supplementing work undertaken in practical fields of work. The School is divided into eleven sections:

General Anthroposophical Section
Section for Mathematics and Astronomy
Medical Section
Natural Science Section
Section for Agriculture
Pedagogical Section
Art Section
Section for the Spiritual Striving of Youth,
    or Youth Section for short
Section for the Art of Eurythmy, Speech, Drama
    and Music
Section for the Literary Arts and Humanities
Section for the Social Sciences

The work in the sections is focused on research, the sharing of ideas and experience, publication, and maintaining links between the activity of the sections and the practical application of anthroposophy in the work of the diverse institutions for anthroposophically-related medicine, education, agriculture, banking etc. all over the

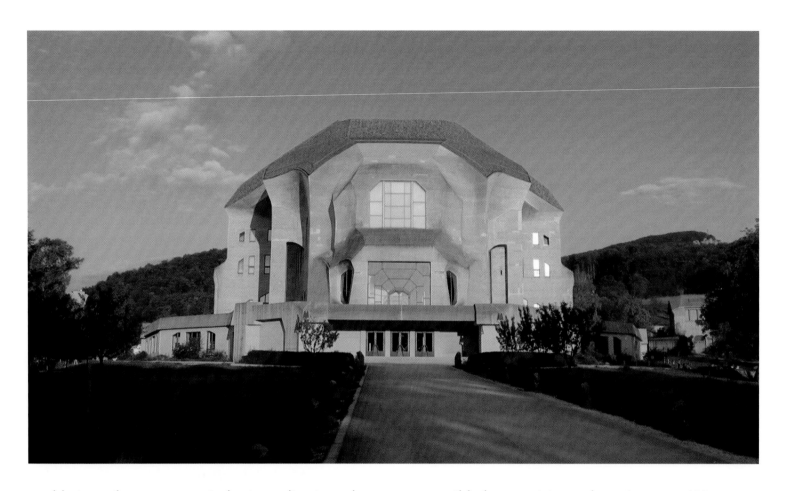

world. Apart from a course in basic studies in anthroposophy held in German and English, an art studies year and the training in speech and drama, basic professional training is not offered at the Goetheanum itself but in facilities throughout the world as well as in the direct vicinity of the Goetheanum itself (College for Anthroposophical Education, Seminar for Curative Education, eurythmy schools, sculpting schools, painting schools, etc.). Alongside research, work in the sections also includes maintaining contact with people working in the various fields of activity who seek to share their ideas and experience. As a consequence, the sections are currently responsible for organising and running some 160 courses and conferences each year. These can range – to give but a few examples – from small conferences on issues relating to beekeeping, for instance, or the special problems arising in tumour research, the specific attributes of money for banking specialists, or a historical survey of scholasticism, to major multi-lingual specialist congresses for teachers at Rudolf Steiner and Waldorf schools, physicians, architects, farmers, people working in curative education, or eurythmists.

All of this requires an operation which can provide space and infrastructure, ensure the dissemination and publication of information (documentation, bookshop, the weekly journal *Das Goetheanum* and the publisher Verlag am Goetheanum), and which can organise catering and accommodation. Depending on the number and timing of events held on the stage and in the sections at any given time, the number of staff at the Goetheanum fluctuates between 200 and 270 people.

How is all of this financed? The annual budget of the General Anthroposophical Society currently comprises some 20–22 million Swiss francs per annum. About half of this is covered by operating income (admission fees, publications, guided tours, etc.), almost a quarter from members' contributions from around the world, and the final quarter from donations and legacies. Unbudgeted building renovations and new building projects are additionally and exclusively financed through donations and legacies.

Many other anthroposophical institutions and facilities with a connection of one kind or another to the Goetheanum have developed in the local area of Dornach and Arlesheim – schools, residential homes, the training facilities already mentioned, trading and manufacturing companies as well as craft and artisan businesses. The best known of these are the pharmaceutical company Weleda AG, the Ita Wegman Clinic and the Lukas Clinic in Arlesheim. Then there is the Rudolf Steiner Nachlassverwaltung which manages Rudolf Steiner's estate, the Rudolf Steiner Verlag publishing house, the Albert Steffen Foundation as well as other foundations. They are linked by their common basis in anthroposophy; but – with few exceptions – all these various facilities and institutions are legally independent of one another.

The building

The Goetheanum was built from 1925–1928 on the basis of a model made by Rudolf Steiner, the founder of anthroposophy. In many respects it was an extraordinary pioneering feat for the time. It is one of the first twentieth-century buildings of this size to be built in concrete and designed in freely sculpted forms which are more than purely utilitarian. The section on the history of the first Goetheanum explains how the stylistic elements of the building must be seen in an historical context of architectural development. Yet the Goetheanum also represents the start of an independent direction within organic architecture which, as anthroposophically-orientated building design, continued to develop throughout the twentieth century. One visible sign of this are the hundred or so buildings in the environs of the Goetheanum in Dornach and Arlesheim, as well as buildings throughout the world. Besides its architecture, the Goetheanum also represented a special pioneering feat in the 1920s in terms of its engineering and construction work. The building engineer, Ole Falk Ebbell, a Norwegian who had his engineering office in Basle and was one of the first great specialists in concrete buildings, openly admitted that he had frequently doubted whether the building could be realised, believing that he had reached the limits of his capacities – and yet he succeeded. Reinforced concrete was still in its infancy at the time, and the Goetheanum illustrated the potential which lay in its use.

The building also represented an incredible feat because a relatively small number of anthroposophists

Why did Rudolf Steiner wish to build in concrete? Why not in the much more living material of wood, as in the first Goetheanum?
Apart from the issue of fire prevention – the first Goetheanum, built in wood, had fallen victim to the flames – Rudolf Steiner was fascinated by reinforced concrete because of the opportunities it offered for unrestricted design. The tensile force of the iron and the compressive strength of the mineral form a polar combination which enables concrete to be poured into the most daring of forms. This makes it a material of unprecedented artistic freedom of expression in architecture. The much-voiced dislike of concrete today is connected less with the material itself than with the dismal way in which it has frequently been used in the course of the twentieth century.

succeeded in realising such a mighty building – and in doing so before the great economic crisis, the world-shattering events of national socialism and the Second World War occurred. The latter factors would probably have made the construction of the building at a later time impossible.

Yet when about 2000 people from all over the world came for the inauguration of the building at the end of September 1928 – all performances, concerts, addresses and lectures had to be held twice – the building was little

more than a shell made temporarily habitable. The building had windows, doors, temporary floors, heating, seating in the main auditorium and some theatre equipment – but everything else was still unfinished. What we see today as the interior finish was undertaken sometime between 1928 and the present day. As late as the early sixties, planks covered in concrete dust and nails from the construction period still ran between the bare concrete pillars in the middle foyer – and that was the cloakroom. Completion of the south stairwell can serve as an example for the rest: in 1930 it was finished as far as the second floor where the main auditorium is situated, by 1951 it had progressed to the fifth floor and in 1993 it had finally reached the top, on the seventh floor. The colours on the walls followed in 2005. We could similarly specify when each space and corner was finished and, indeed, when any renovation was undertaken which had become necessary in the interim. One single section has remained unfinished to the present day: the north-east stairwell behind the stage which is used only by staff and is still awaiting completion.

Why has building work continued over such a long period? Why was the Goetheanum not finished in one go?
Building work was only ever undertaken where funding from donations and legacies was available – no debts were ever incurred for the Goetheanum.

The building as an expression of anthroposophy

If we wish to understand the special characteristics of the forms, colours, pictures and structures of the building, we need to take account of the following: philosophical ideas and a particular view of the world are formulated in thoughts and concepts using language, and they address the human being at a particular level of understanding. But if we are dealing with content which goes beyond intellectually comprehensible concepts it can also be expressed through visible forms and artistic creation in a way which is just as meaningful as conceptual formulations. In this sense Greek temples, Gothic cathedrals, classical theatres and modern department stores are the visible expression of a particular kind of religious outlook, an attitude to life, a philosophy or, indeed, a particular view of the world.

The impulse to lend expression to anthroposophy not just in the form of concepts and thoughts through books, lectures and dialogue, but also through artistic creation, underlies the two Goetheanum buildings. The visitor is thereby encouraged to take the forms and colours which he or she sees not as symbols or signs of something else, which in turn have to be interpreted, but as the direct artistic expression of content and processes which can also be expressed in ideas.

A walk around the Goetheanum

The process described here also comes to expression in anthroposophical architecture in metamorphoses, such as can be experienced in many different ways in the Goetheanum building. Metamorphosis is understood as the transformation of a basic form into many further forms of manifestation within the architecture of a single building or within a whole ensemble of buildings. At the same time it means that a building forms a coherent whole in all its parts through such a transmutation of forms.

The first thing we notice as we walk around the building is the difference between the architecture of the eastern section and the forms of the western part. In the east, towards the slopes rising to the Gempenfluh, we have a strict cube, a high straight wall. And if Rudolf Steiner had not agreed during the planning-approval process to respond to the wishes of the Goetheanum's neighbours in Arlesheim to soften these severe lines a little, the corners of the building would have been left without their corner pilasters and roof cornices. To the west, in contrast, we have an exceedingly dynamic free form that falls in cascades and flows out into the surrounding area, welcoming approaching visitors to the building.

Like a counterpoint we have in the east many apparently disparate symmetrical windows which, on closer inspection, turn out to be like a lens allowing us to see through the building to the west façade. And on the west façade, the severely right-angled entrance section, the large, almost square portal on the terrace, and the equally severe form of the upper west window appear like a view through the building to the east façade. In the Goetheanum's east section where the stage is situated, where speakers deliver their lectures, and where artists prepare themselves for their performance, the focus is on what happens inside in an inner protected space – expressed through a severe, almost repelling form towards the exterior. In the west, however, everyone is warmly invited to enter. Here the important aspect is the connection between outer and inner, between inner and outer.

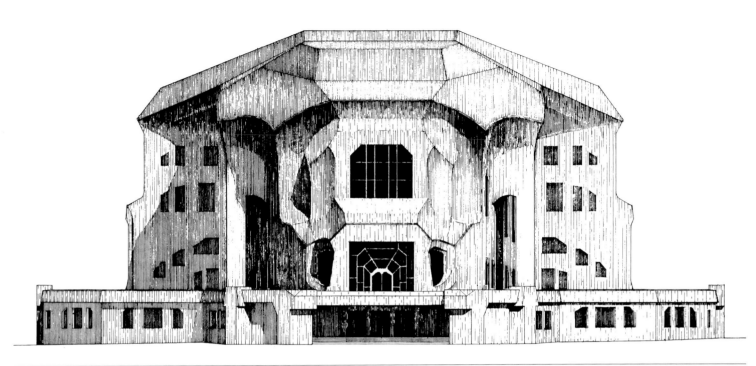

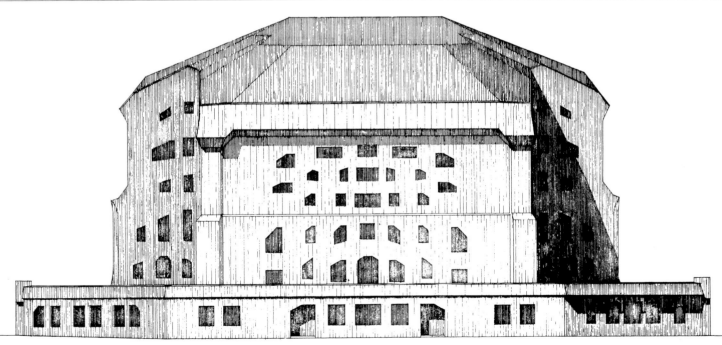

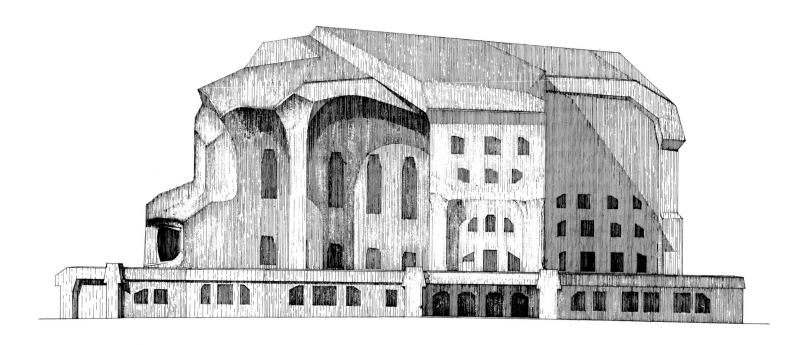

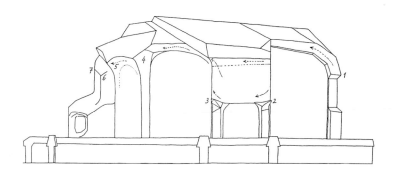

These aspects create the architectural task of combining two opposing elements. A look at the south or north façade reveals how Rudolf Steiner solved this challenge. What starts in the south-eastern corner with the severe-shaped pilaster is gradually transformed. We begin with the pilaster in its simple form (1); at the two corners of the south wing (2 and 3) it turns into an increasingly elaborate half pillar; the fourth step (4) is revealed as a free standing pillar, and with the dynamic lines over the west façade (5–7) the form begins increasingly to dissolve. The contrasting forms are evident even in the shuttering boards. Long, broad planks were used for the shuttering in the eastern sections of the building whereas it is evident from the small, often curved and bent small planks for the shuttering of the west that the foreman in charge had learned his trade in the ship building industry and was using the techniques learned there for the flowing forms of the west section.

Observed from a distance, we can see how the same formal motif appears in the landscape: rising from the river Birs valley towards the Gempenfluh, the natural forms become increasingly pronounced until the slope – no longer visible from Dornach – meets a steep rock face towards the east. In this way the Goetheanum takes up the forms of the landscape and enhances them artistically. Rudolf Steiner himself said that, having lived in Dornach for ten years, he was able to take account of the landscape in designing the model for the second building in quite a different way from the first Goetheanum. We will see in the chapter on the first building, which burnt down in 1922, how its forms could be placed anywhere in the world – but the shapes of the second building belong to the place where they were built, they have grown out of the landscape.

The Goetheanum could not have been better located: it is situated neither down on the plain nor on top of a mountain but in a wonderful intermediate position on a rising slope. It is neither in the city nor in the wilds, but near the historic cultural centre of Basle. In addition, it is of the greatest significance that it is located in Switzerland and not in its northern neighbour, where it was originally to have been built. This enabled it to avoid destruction despite the events of the twentieth century.

But let us return to the forms visible from the outside. The auditorium with its high windows is clearly recognisable in the west, as is the stage section with its adjacent cloakrooms and storage rooms in the east. Separating, yet also linking the east and west sections we have the two wings towards north and south, which on the one hand contain stairwells and conference rooms and on the other hand the stage extensions. All of these spaces rest on a terrace surrounding the whole under which various rooms are situated. There is also a mezzanine floor on the level of the terrace and the auditorium where the offices of the executive council are now situated.

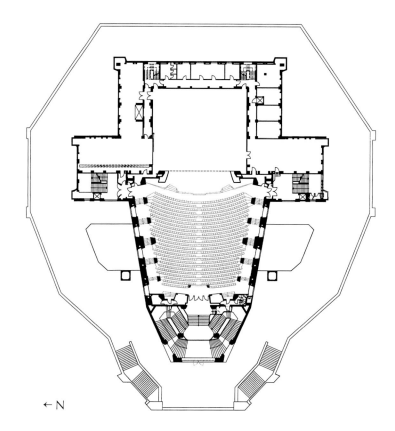

← N

The creation of the second Goetheanum

Before moving on to a description of the interior of the Goetheanum, let us take a look at its history. We have to imagine that after the fire which destroyed the first wooden Goetheanum during the night of New Year 1922/23 little remained on the Dornach hill other than a heap of rubble. A work which had been built with tremendous commitment in the years from 1913 to 1920 had been destroyed. The rich artistic design of the carved pillars and architraves, the painted ceiling, the ground stained-glass windows – all of those things had become no more than a memory. Indeed, the Anthroposophical Society itself was little more than a heap of rubble in which rivalries, a lack of clear structures and an absence of cooperation made the focus on common goals almost impossible. In addition, there was a hostile attitude towards anthroposophy, promoted by a variety of groups ranging from theosophical circles, representatives of the Catholic Church and Protestant pastors to nationalist associations and, in Germany, the rise of national socialism. As a consequence there were many people who were pleased about the fire at the first Goetheanum and who, in individual cases, went as far as to sabotage attempts to fight the fire.

Given these circumstances, Rudolf Steiner's primary concern was to stop the anthroposophical movement from breaking apart. In the course of 1923 new structures and relations were gradually established which led to the re-founding of the Anthroposophical Society at Christmas 1923 and the international union of national anthroposophical societies which had been established in various parts of the world. It makes sense that a building such as the second Goetheanum can only be built on the basis of a strong social structure. During the founding meeting of the new society Rudolf Steiner for the first time set out his ideas for rebuilding the Goetheanum, and produced the blackboard drawing shown below, in his lecture of 1 January 1924.

In the following weeks, ideas about the new building grew more detailed and specific. In March 1924 Rudolf Steiner withdrew from all commitments for three days to work in his studio in the carpentry building, next to the burnt-out ruin, on the model on which the new architectural designs were to be based. The model which Steiner then had taken to the architects' office in the Glass House must have come as a mighty shock to them: how were they to transform these completely novel forms into a building made of concrete, on a scale of 100:1?

A phase of intensive planning, study of design variations, and negotiations with the authorities began. It was necessary to allow for the fact that establishment of the School of Spiritual Science within the Anthroposophical Society during the Christmas conference had considerably increased spatial requirements from those of the first Goetheanum. In contrast to 1913, when no planning laws yet existed in Dornach, the new building was subject to approval by the authorities. The building application was made as early as June 1924. In fierce campaigns, those opposed to the rebuilding of the Goetheanum attempted to use all their leverage with the government of the canton of Solothurn to prevent it going ahead. Submissions referred to the need for spiritual and cultural protection of the homeland against what was referred to as contamination by foreign influences. But protection of the homeland in an aesthetic sense was also demanded. That simply meant assimilation with existing building designs in as unobtrusive a way as possible and on no scale grander than could be grasped by a parochial mind. But the local council in Dornach, under its mayor Bernhard Krauss, and some cantonal deputies together with almost 200 signatories from Dornach voiced their committed support – in a way which showed they understood the wider implications for the state. A submission to the cantonal government on the issue of spiritual and cultural protection of the homeland stated that "Freedom of confession and belief as one of the highest ideals of our state prohibits any kind of suppression or persecution of our fellow human beings with differing views, even if we do not understand the teachings of the anthroposophists and, in so far as we do understand them, disagree with them. [...] However, it seems wholly impermissible to us, indeed almost frivolous, to appeal to feelings of patriotism, of remembrance of our forefathers

and veneration of our freedom fighters, in order to engage in suppression of the free spiritual and cultural activity for which they fought, and to remove the presence of people with views different to our own." A further comment on the aesthetic issue runs as follows: "The issue of the beauty of a given work is more controversial than ever today. [...] A building with such a purpose and, as a consequence, such dimensions, cannot be built in the style of our residential buildings. It cannot be inconspicuously hidden. Its critics would no doubt be at a loss to know how to create a design which both conforms to their criteria yet also fulfils the sentiment and purpose of the society undertaking the building – which is to bear prime responsibility for financing it and which therefore has the overriding right to determine its design." The subsequent argument that the St. Ursen cathedral in Solothurn does not correspond to the surrounding houses in style or size either is a point

exquisitely made. "As soon as the community of anthroposophists is granted the right to its own way of thinking and perception, it must also be granted the additional right to choose a form of building in keeping with that way of thinking. That this will not be a form commonly found in our country is self-evident."

In the end, only the height of the building was slightly reduced at the request of the authorities together with a few other small changes. A change in the form of the roof resulted from detailed study of the technical requirements for the stage, with regard to the height of the flies. The structural calculations were checked by an independent engineer. Once a second building application was submitted, the government approved the building plans as early as November 1924. The demolition work on the ruins of the first Goetheanum began in the winter of 1924/25. In the meantime it had been realised that the concrete ter-

race would have to be demolished as well since it was too damaged to serve as a terrace for the second building as had initially been assumed.

In the meantime, Rudolf Steiner had become seriously ill and had to work on the further development of the building plans from his sick bed. He died on 30 March 1925 while the demolition work was still going on. As a result he was only involved in the plans for the exterior form of the building. Interior completion of the building was still undecided at his death. He only made very few suggestions in this respect. He was aware that a building built once cannot be repeated and that a new building has to respond to the contemporary situation. That the second Goetheanum is so clearly distinct from the first one is also connected with the fact that the spiritual situation in Europe had completely changed since the First World War. Nothing was the same as before. In the works of

other architects before and after the First World War, too, we can experience the depth of this change. And yet a closer study reveals how the two Goetheanum buildings are connected in their inner structure, how the second building is a metamorphosis of the first one. We will return to this theme in the chapter on the first Goetheanum.

Building work proceeded apace. For this purpose the administration of the Goetheanum building had expanded its own team to the not inconsiderable number of 120 workers and formed its own building company. As early as 29 September 1926 the topping out ceremony took place; on 18 July 1927 the great wooden carving of the Representative of Humanity, described below, was set up in the room designated for that purpose; and on 29 September 1928 the official opening took place. The photos illustrate the events more clearly than words. They also show that the technical equipment used for the building

21

was far simpler than today. There were no cranes, no steel scaffolding, no vibrators to compact the cement. The prepared concrete was carried up the scaffolding in large containers by the workers and compacted between the shuttering with long wooden poles. Sand, gravel and concrete, delivered by railway to the station at Dornach-Arlesheim, was taken to the building site by local farmers using horse and cart. And the building site was constantly threatened by the sword of Damocles of inadequate funds. The financial basis was provided by the insurance money for the first building. But that was only a beginning. Donations had to be collected slowly and gradually. The situation became critical in 1927 – the west façade had not yet been built and there was some doubt as to whether the building work could continue. The treasurer of the society at the time, Dr. Guenther Wachsmuth, took a trip to visit national societies and branches and report on the building. He returned with the necessary money to complete its outer shell.

Let us now take a walk through the various areas of the Goetheanum.

Some figures at this point:

Greatest length: 92 m with terrace
Greatest length of the superstructure: 72 m
Greatest width with terrace: 85 m
Greatest width of superstructure: 64 m
Greatest height: 37 m
Interior space: 110,000 m³,
   corresponding to approx. 160 medium-sized single family houses
Concrete used: 15,000 m³
Building cost in Swiss francs at the time:
   approx. 7 million, corresponding in today's money to approximately 14 times that amount.

The west staircase

The visitor enters the middle foyer, passing through the three mighty portals of the west entrance to the cloak-rooms below the main auditorium. During conferences, visitor reception and the information table are situated here. The west staircase ascends in a great arc. Halfway up the right staircase, anyone going up will meet the people ascending the left staircase, and at the top at the entrance to the auditorium they meet again. These curved paths, with the absence of any functional linearity, on which people keep re-encountering one another, begin well before the front of the west entrance: the path from the Speisehaus restaurant, the so-called *Felsliweg*, leads the visitor to a first view of the building, hides it again and then makes it reappear. The path invites the visitor to stand back before approaching the building in a straight line. This is a first example of the way in which the architecture of this building is not solely restricted to fulfilling a purpose but takes as its subject human beings with their experience, their searches and encounters.

In the summer and during major performances, the large portal to the terrace halfway up to the auditorium is opened and invites the visitor to take a stroll around the building. It is as if on the way to the theatre people have already liberated themselves a little from the earth or – during the interval – do not need to return fully to every-day reality. It is something special when, during the interval, particular moods of nature can be experienced here, especially in the summer when the sun sets in the West towards the Vosges mountains.

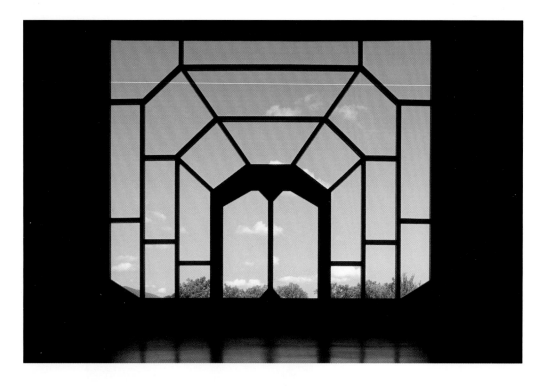

Returning from the terrace door to the staircase, the visitor sees a large sculpture by Günter Oling on the landing and a large figure of Michael by Walther Kniebe above the corridor entrance.

Looking upwards to the dome of the stairwell, the visitor can see very clearly the concrete structure which was required to provide the necessary support for the flowing external forms.

The path continues upwards, with the staircase arcing symmetrically in an S-shape on both sides. Standing before the doors to enter the auditorium, we sense a rosy light behind us and turn round once more. We see – depending on the intensity of the sunlight – the rays of a shining carmine: the first of nine stained glass windows describing the path of the human being to higher knowledge. We will talk more about that in a separate chapter.

The main auditorium

Let us start by looking at the shape of the auditorium. A trapeze opening out towards the stage forms the basic shape of the auditorium, whereas the stage itself is essentially a square. These two shapes intersect by the width of the proscenium. An unusual feature here is the fact that the trapeze opens out towards the front. This gives the auditorium a perspective effect, leaving the audience, even in the back rows, with the impression of being quite near to the stage; the distance to the stage appears foreshortened by the diverging walls. Conversely, the speaker on the proscenium or the actor on the stage has the impression that the audience at the back of the auditorium is not that far away. From this perspective it comes almost as a surprise that the auditorium has seating for a thousand people.

This shape of an intersecting trapeze and square is a metamorphosis of the form which the first Goetheanum embodied in its dual cupolas. In the first building, the auditorium and the stage related much more directly to one another since the stage, too, had been artistically finished down to the last detail. It also had carved plinths, capitals, architraves and a painted ceiling like the larger domed space. The decision to install a technically-equipped stage in the rebuilt second Goetheanum meant an absence of this artistic whole, created through sculpture and painting, in the relationship between auditorium and stage. What remained was the relationship between the auditorium and the stage in terms of its basic layout – and the challenge to achieve the effect produced through

sculpted and painted design in the original building by means of stage craft and stage design.

The auditorium was used in its unfinished state for almost thirty years. Apart from a very simple barrel vault made from a thin suspended plaster ceiling which covered the roof structures, the bare concrete walls were visible everywhere. The wood used during construction for the shuttering and scaffolding was turned into flooring still impregnated with cement dust. Only one thing installed at the beginning has survived the test of time, although renovated and improved in design: the 1000 seats made of elm wood which were donated by Czech friends. In the 1930s the glass windows were added and the organ in the 1950s. Both glass windows and organ have been reinstalled today.

In 1957 the auditorium was completed for the first time, with walls executed in simple forms using the Rabitz technique and a suspended ceiling which started out as white but turned increasingly grey, and which at the time was unfortunately made of asbestos. Based on a competition of ideas among a number of invited architects, the executive council at the Goetheanum decided in lonely splendour to base the execution of the work on a model by Prof. Johannes Schöpfer from Stuttgart (1892–1961). But his design was very controversial and led to difficult and ugly disputes within the Anthroposophical Society. Key aspects of the concept underlying the building appeared to have been left out of consideration. And yet the people in charge at the time, Albert Steffen and Guenther Wachsmuth, were responding to a need to complete the interior of the building. The subsequent generation, which became acquainted with the Goetheanum in the following decades – including the author of this booklet – knew nothing about these difficulties and lived with the auditorium as the best possible version at the time. But when in the 1980s – the harmful nature of asbestos having been proven – the authorities intensified their demands for the asbestos ceiling to be removed, people began to think again about the issues which had been raised previously. The need to completely replace the ceiling, the inadequacy of heating, ventilation and lighting equipment, the fact that the 1957 completion of the auditorium had done nothing to improve acoustics, and the unsatisfactory nature of architectural features – all of these things led, during a lengthy planning period starting in 1989, to a decision to gut the auditorium down to its shell and completely redesign it. This work was accomplished between 1996 and 1998.

The first step on this path was taken with the appointment of Christian Hitsch, a sculptor and painter who was the director of an art school in Vienna at the time, as head of the Art Section within the School of Spiritual Science.

The appointment included the express instruction to embark on redesigning the auditorium. With the greatest energy and perseverance he began to investigate various approaches in a series of what, in the end, became twelve model designs. But all of them shared the basic idea of metamorphosis through seven plinths, capitals and pillars as well as the architrave above them, as originally undertaken in the first Goetheanum. Rudolf Steiner had attempted to execute such a metamorphosis of forms through seven stages, both in the first Goetheanum and also, in a rudimentary way, in the design of a conference hall in Munich as early as 1907, and in a further two attempts in Stuttgart and Malsch. Christian Hitsch was convinced that buildings such as the Goetheanum – which is ultimately intended to be a mystery site and not just any building serving a merely functional purpose – require this kind of metamorphosis of forms as a basic stylistic element whose significance extends far into the future.

A further motif is the integration of the arts into a total work of art, an ideal for which many an architect was striving at the start of the twentieth century, but which was satisfactorily accomplished only in the rarest of cases. Architecture, sculpture and painting should combine in the total work of art in such a way that one arises from the other and that all three elements arise out of the same spirit. Within a total work of art conceived in this way, what happens as drama, as language and music made visible through movement in eurythmy, and, finally, what is spoken, experienced and thought in the auditorium, is part of the whole. The idea is thus to avoid "just" creating architecture and then "beautifying" it with art as a kind of after-thought, using any money that might be spare – as happens so often. On the contrary, architecture, sculpture and painting must interact right from the beginning. The fact that Christian Hitsch, a sculptor with building experience and a talent for painting, was commissioned

to undertake the initial planning, was an expression of this.

But the sculptor also needed an architect and so Ulrich Oelssner was found. Based in Stuttgart, he had designed many buildings, including, in particular, churches for the Christian Community. From a certain stage onwards they collaborated on developing the plans, although it very soon became clear that a third person was also needed, namely an acoustics engineer. Such a person was found in the engineer Jörg Kümmel from the Müller-BBM acoustics office in Munich. The key development work was thus undertaken in a cooperative effort between a sculptor, architect and acoustical engineer. The acoustical engineer was dissatisfied with the designs for a long time and said that good acoustics would not be achieved in the way being pursued, since the sculptural designs which – in the initial plans – were intended to go on the walls in the form of reliefs, left a great distance between the walls. The breakthrough to a solution which satisfied all three parties did not occur until the first weeks of 1995, when the idea was adopted of erecting pillars at a little distance from the walls. This made it possible to considerably reduce the interior space determining the acoustics, in other words, the distance from wall to wall and proportionately to the ceiling. In this way the risk of causing echoes could be avoided. At the same time acoustically reflective materials were used everywhere. This last point was decisive in relation to the planned painting of the ceiling since a painting can only be made on a reflecting, i.e. hard surface.

The design with seven pillars on each of the side walls, with the first and the seventh pillars merging into the corners of the auditorium, leaving five free-standing pillars, was very much in the spirit of the metamorphic concept of sculptural forms in the first Goetheanum; but it also gave rise to renewed criticism that the project was merely recycling an old architectural idea dating back decades. Critics who argue this fail to understand that the forms created in the first Goetheanum are deeper in meaning than mere fashions outdated after a few decades. In Gothic architecture, for example, it would not have occurred to anyone to criticise a building for imitating another one 80 years earlier, since the spirituality which comes to expression in the Gothic style developed over a longer period. Similarly, building design permeated by anthroposophical spirituality cannot be subject to rapidly-changing architectural fashions – which might continually produce new and "original" designs, but which equally quickly lose their significance.

A language of forms for the new sculptural design of the interior space was needed, which embodied the change in style from the first to the second Goetheanum, the change from wood to concrete. This is more than just a change of materials, involving the change from rounded, curved forms to a more angular element, which wakens consciousness to a greater extent. Attempts to have the new walls carved in wood again were unsatisfactory. But how can concrete, the modern material of the second building, be used for sculpted design of its interior?

The solution was found in shotcrete (sprayed concrete). There was, however, no experience of using shotcrete as the basis for sculptural work on interior spaces. The specialist companies for shotcrete within a radius of 300 kilometres were invited to develop the equipment and composition for an appropriate type of concrete in cooperation with a small research group

headed by Tobias Nöthiger, a young craftsman and artist of great initiative who died shortly after completion of the building. A small company from Ticino, Laich SA, headed by Pietro Teichert, turned out to possess the necessary skills. As a result, the walls were made from a shotcrete with special characteristics which was much lighter than ordinary concrete because pumice was added instead of pebbles, and made easier for sculptors to work with through the addition of chalk. The concrete had a warm reddish colour through the addition of iron oxide, i.e. rust in pulverised form.

The individual steps in the construction of such walling are, briefly, as follows:

- A strong steel structure bears and supports the walls.
- A team of artists and craftsmen pre-form the iron core grid for the walls, corresponding to the model of the walls, in a rented factory hall.
- The iron sculpture of the wall core grid is taken to the building site in manageable sections and anchored into the steel structure.
- The core grid is supplemented on site and backed with expanded metal.
- Shotcrete is applied in three layers. A further grid made of glass fibre nets is inserted between the second and third layers. The overall thickness of the wall is approx. 10–12 cm. During the concreting process, staff from the shotcrete company work together with an artist.
- Once the walls have dried and hardened, sculptural work starts on the previously pre-formed walls. One to three centimetres of the concrete surface are removed in this process. The sculptors do not work with hammer and chisel but with axes. Forty to fifty sculptors and assistants work on this design for the next six months. The job of the assistants is to keep disposing of the chippings.

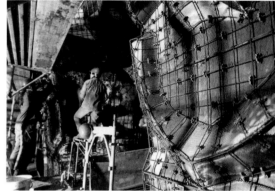

The work community

The major project of renovating the auditorium from 1996 to 1998 would not have been possible if the huge financial resources supplied by the anthroposophical movement had not been supplemented by the work of hundreds of friends who gave active help on the building site. The result was a collaboration between workers from a great variety of specialist firms and artists and helpers from among our own ranks, giving the building site its own special character. There were always about 100 people at work throughout the 20-month construction period. Some came for the whole period of sculptural work, or when the doors were carved; others stayed for two weeks to take on the daily cleaning tasks on the building site or to assist plasterers, etc. The workers from specialist firms together with helpers from the anthroposophical movement produced an internationally diverse work community, based on shared love of this building and a high level of commitment. Additional support came from several firms agreeing to undertake large parts of the job on a "scheduled work" basis, i.e. they were just paid for actual time and materials, rather than on the basis of an all-inclusive or flat-rate price. This is not usual on large construction sites but it accorded with the special challenges of this unusual building project.

The three motifs of development

As already discussed when we first examined the exterior form of the Goetheanum, metamorphosis as an expression of a path of evolution and development is an essential element of anthroposophical architecture. The main auditorium contains three elements representing evolution. The sculptural design of the walls with the seven pillars, capitals and architraves gives us an image of cosmic evolution. The painted ceiling represents motifs of human evolution, from the Creation to the present, and the images in the stained glass windows describe the path of the individual human being and his development to higher knowledge.

All three evolutionary motifs hark back to the representations in the first Goetheanum which prefigure them, and thus to the sketches and suggestions of Rudolf Steiner. And all three have been reworked, reinterpreted and individually designed throughout by the artists undertaking the work in such a way that they form a unity with the forms of the second Goetheanum building. One of the most important reasons for the renovation of the auditorium in the 1990s was to facilitate, once again, an experience of this trinity of evolutionary motifs. Let us look at them in greater detail.

Cosmic evolution – sculptural design of the walls

Rudolf Steiner draws on his spiritual research to describe the evolutionary phases of our planet earth. He shows how the earth has, in infinitely long periods, solidified through purely spiritual forces from an entity initially existing only as warmth into a body condensed to air, and further into watery, jelly-like matter, eventually becoming what we know today as our mineral-based, solid earth. Between these four stages from – in simple terms – warmth via air and water to earth, there were long periods in which each phase of development disintegrated again or, to put it a different way, was transformed back into purely spiritual qualities. Borrowing from ancient esoteric traditions, Rudolf Steiner called these different phases by the names of the seven planets, although they are not directly connected with the planets we see today. Thus we have passed through Saturn – Sun – Moon – Earth. Looking into the future, there will be three further stages: Jupiter – Venus – Vulcan. In the sculptural representation of the capitals, the final cosmic state of Vulcan has been omitted and the earth has been presented in two sections, which we might call Mars and Mercury, so that the sequence of planetary states as an image of cosmic evolution can be presented in the following order: Saturn – Sun – Moon – Mars – Mercury – Jupiter – Venus. We can also call these stages planetary incarnations. The fact that there are seven stages is not connected with any particular symbolism or mysticism. If we study any kind of developmental process we will see that development invariably and naturally occurs in seven stages. There is a good reason

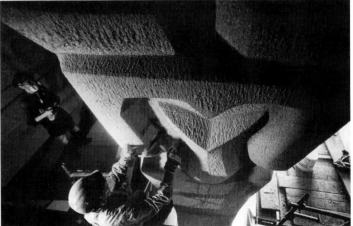

why the week is divided into seven days, which are assigned to the planets in the same sequence – something we find reflected in many languages. These seven stages of planetary evolution are represented in the seven pillars with their capitals and plinths.

But we can also look at the capitals and architraves from the point of view of their artistic metamorphosis and avoid a conceptual explanation altogether. Thus we can observe them as purely sculptural forms and concentrate on how the forms are transformed from one to the next. Each form captures a new stage of the transformation process, but the metamorphosis itself occurs in the invisible space between the visible forms; we might say, in the depths of the lacuna which is a "void" between the pillars – in which something important occurs invisibly. The sequence starts in the rear corner of the auditorium with a relatively simple form in which a point from above approaches a point from below. This simple form becomes more complex and dynamic in the next two pillars and in the fourth pillar something new altogether is added which continues to develop. The fifth form appears confusing in its diversity, with the snake-like form winding around a central rod. By the seventh form, things have become simplified again, but at a higher level. A new cycle of development could start from this point.

Development of humanity – the painted ceiling

Humanity today is developing in the phase which we described within cosmic evolution as the incarnation of the earth. Innumerable myths and sagas as well as religious documents describe the origin of the earth. Common to all of them is that the driving force which created the earth came from spiritual beings. Rather than the Big Bang or a physically determined event which occurred at the beginning, God or the Elohim or other gods or beings set things in motion. They created human beings and with them the animals, plants and, indeed, everything lifeless as well. The painted ceiling starts above the gallery with the representation of such events in a deep blue colour. Eyes and ears are the human organs which belong to this aspect of creation and give human beings access to the earth. Everything still happens in the unity between the divine and the human, as expressed in the image of paradise. But this unity is sundered through the serpent's temptation, and the human being becomes independent, separate in his consciousness from the beings who created him. In primeval times, long before historical or geological and archaeological records tell of human beings, the earth looked quite different. Rudolf Steiner's spiritual research tells of Lemuria, a fiery, constantly transforming territory in today's region of the Indian Ocean. This land perished in disastrous fires. The next evolutionary phase of humanity occurred with Atlantis, the mythical territory between Africa, Europe and America, which ended in the disaster of the Flood. And then the cultural epochs begin which move closer to our own time and for which we

have the first historical indications: the high cultures of India and Persia, followed by Mesopotamia and Egypt, Greece and Rome to the present day. The gestures of I – A – O challenge us to unite the forces of thinking, feeling and will, which are fragmenting in our time, into a unity guided by the ego.

The images stop with the present – the future lies beyond the threshold on the stage. In the first Goetheanum the images of the great cupola continued in the smaller cupola, where painted motifs pointed towards the future: Faust's quest; coming to terms with the forces of evil; Christ, who gave humanity the strength for future development. The motif of Christ painted in the cupola continues what should have stood beneath it in the form of a large sculpture (see the chapter on the Representative of Humanity, page 87).

The motifs of the ceiling paintings

1   The Elohim create the earth, the beings of light radiate
2   The senses are born, the eye and the ear
3   Jahve and the Temptation of Lucifer – the paradise
4   Lemuria
5   Atlantis
6   The Indian man
7   The Persian man
8   The Egyptian man
9   Greece and the motif of Oedipus
10 The Anger of God and the Sadness of God – the I
11 The Dance of the Seven – the A
12 The Circle of the Twelve – the O

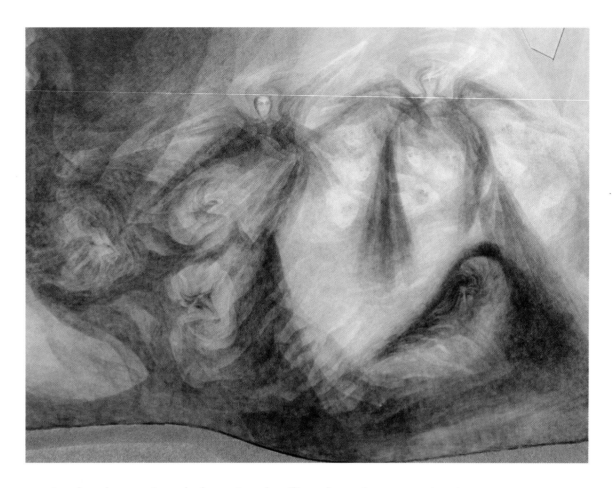

As already mentioned, the painted ceiling draws its inspiration from sketches prepared by Rudolf Steiner for the cupolas of the first Goetheanum. In preparatory work for redesigning the main auditorium, a larger group of painters, who repeatedly met at the Goetheanum, studied possible designs for the ceiling. One of the things which was examined was whether other motifs might be depicted – the archangels, the zodiac or the seasons of the year. But the group always returned to the motifs from the first Goetheanum. They seemed just right for this location. But uncertainty persisted until building began as to whether the painted ceiling could be realised and would receive the necessary support – not least financial. In our time, just as in other historical periods, there are people who wish to live without images, who oppose them or are, indeed, iconoclastic because they would rather have solely inner religious experiences, and feel perturbed by outer pictures depicting spiritual dimensions. But in the end the conviction prevailed that the design of the walls and the stained glass windows should be supplemented by a painted ceiling as third element, as in the first Goetheanum.

Out of the larger gathering of painters there crystallised a smaller group of seven painters who were now to undertake the mighty job of painting 560 m² of ceiling. They were given three months. But up on the scaffolding they were so close to the large depictions that it was impossible to gain an overview of the whole. That is why everything depended on proper preparation of the work. For a whole year the painters practised painting above their heads, studied the composition of the whole, painted the whole ceiling twice on a scale of 1:2, and learned to handle the plant colours produced by Günter Meier and his assistants in his own laboratory at the Goetheanum. All of this took place in the factory hall in which the sculptured metal framework for the walls was simultaneously being built.

The ceiling itself is a suspended design consisting of a rough steel grid with reinforcements, measured to the nearest millimetre, which hangs from the roof structure, and a net through which a mixture of plaster, chalk and sand has been sprayed. The reinforcement and the net are approximately in the middle of the 3 or 4 cm-thick ceiling. The whole ceiling, designed in one large section, also had to be sprayed in one go, an outstanding accomplishment by the plastering company which undertook the job in one day with 16 men, starting at six in the morning and finishing at one o'clock the following morning. Once the ceiling had dried, an approximately 10 cm-thick layer of very light insulating material was sprayed on the upper surface facing the roof structure and several layers of primer were applied to the lower surface in preparation for the plant-based paints.

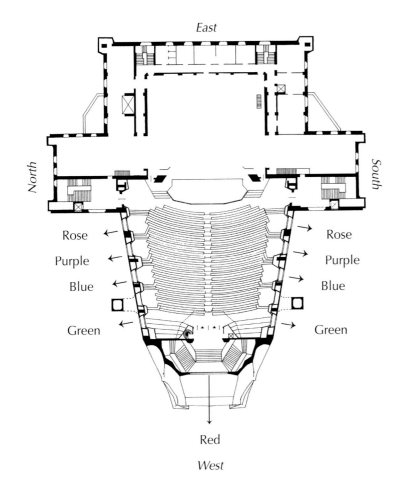

East

North

South

Rose ← → Rose

Purple ← → Purple

Blue ← → Blue

Green ← → Green

Red

West

Individual development – the stained-glass windows

The further that world and earth evolution progresses, the more its focus moves from the development of tribes, peoples, families and cultures to the individual development of each single person. Here the further stages are no longer dependent on creative beings exerting external influence on people, but solely on each person him- or herself. The path which human beings tread in the endeavour for knowledge and self-development is the subject of the stained-glass windows.

The red window

Someone setting out on a path of schooling is initially confronted with the forces arising from his own soul as fear, hate, derision and doubt, embodied in the image of fearsome animals blocking his gaze into spiritual realities (left image). Once these forces have been overcome, there is an open prospect to the beings in spiritual heights (right image). As a person progresses on his path of schooling, his organs of supersensible perception begin to open and become active, represented in the lotus flowers on the forehead and in the region of the larynx. He becomes aware of his connection with the cosmos, indicated by the constellations in the zodiac of Leo and Taurus as well as in Saturn. But such an inner path is not possible without the inner courage indicated, in the simple depiction of Michael with the dragon, in the lowest section.

41

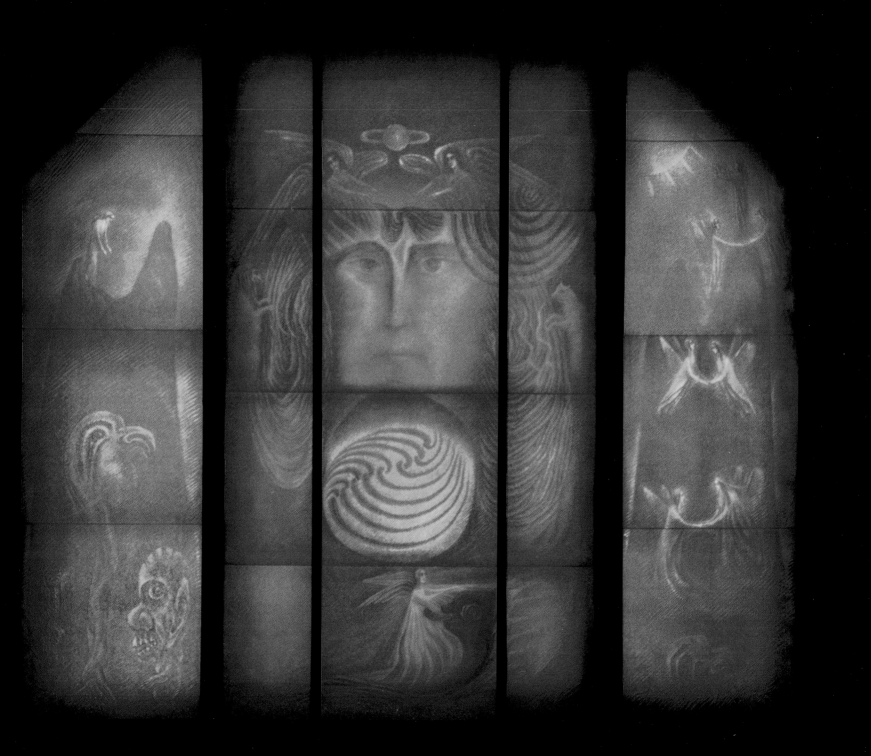

The green windows

The first challenge facing the pupil on his spiritual path is the conflict with evil. It appears in two different forms. On the one hand there is cold, sharp intelligence in the image of the serpent encircling the whole cosmos with piercing eyes and in the image of the elemental beings boring into the earth in the green north window. On the other hand, in the south window there is the enchantingly beautiful angel giving human beings knowledge and independence but also severing their connection with the spiritual world. Both are traditionally described as the devil despite their opposing nature. But earlier names such as devil and Satan, diabolos and satanas, give an indication that their differences were formerly understood. In anthroposophical terminology they are called Ahriman and Lucifer.

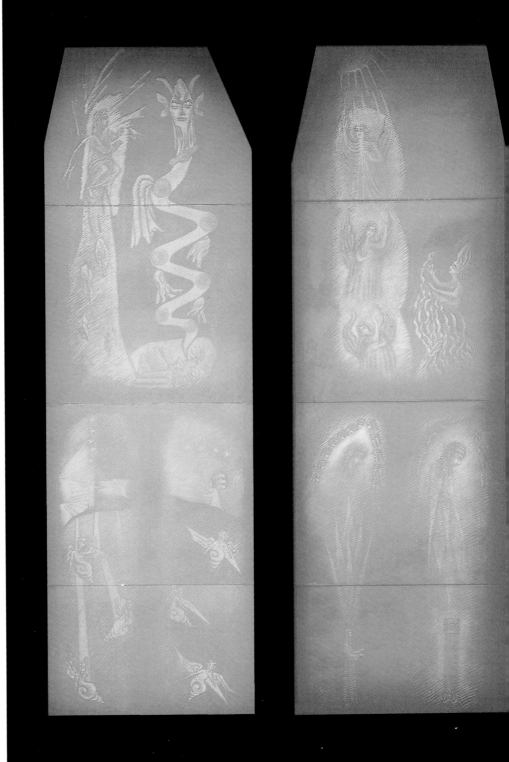

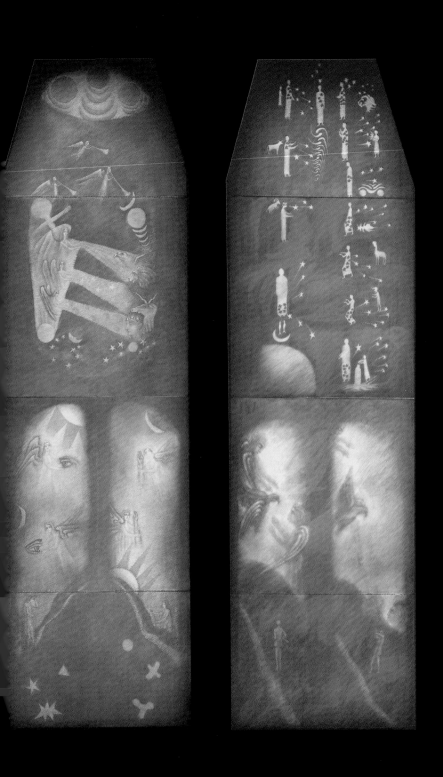

The blue windows

In the next step, the spiritual pupil is immersed in the secrets of the cosmos in which he experiences the connection between the macrocosm and the microcosm. The human body is built from the forces of the Zodiac and the images in the blue south window show in detail where each force of the Zodiac has been active in building the body. The north window, in contrast, shows the connection between the human sense organs and the cosmos, with the eye and the sense of touch representing the other senses.

The purple windows

Here we see the enigma of time, the path of the soul and spirit through time. Rudolf Steiner brought back to awareness something which was taken as self-evident in ancient times, but which had been lost – for good reason – in western cultures, namely the fact that the innermost core of the human being, the spirit soul, inhabits a human body not just once, but incarnates repeatedly over long periods of time. Over a long series of incarnations it can thus acquire abilities and experience, and develop in ways impossible in a single lifetime. Connected with this is the knowledge, which can simultaneously be experienced as a deeply-felt reality of life, that the intrinsic human being, the part of the human being which forms a person's essential "I", is indivisible and indestructible and that our physical existence is simply a garment for this essential core of our being. This process is comparable to the human being putting his clothes on in the morning and taking them off again at night. The purple south window illustrates how the spirit soul sets out from the spiritual world, that is, the world it inhabits between death and a new birth, to enter the physical world. At first, the spirit soul – shown at the very top of the image as a head of Janus – looks back into its past, to what it has acquired, and at the same time it looks into the future, gazing down to the parents who will provide it with a physical embryo. At a soul and

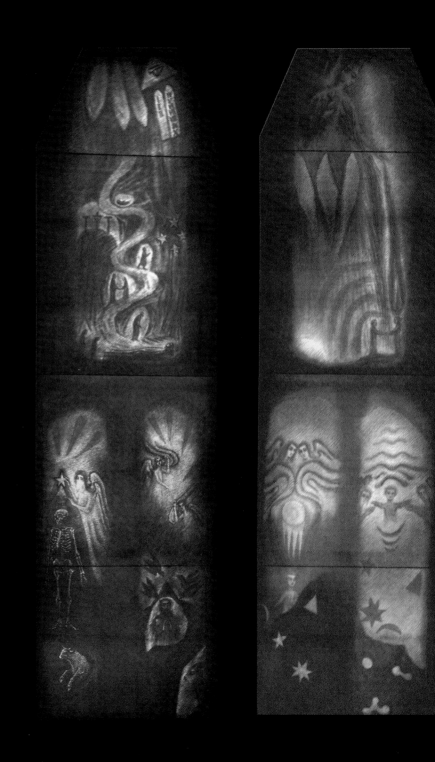

spiritual level, the being preparing to incarnate is already involved in the encounter of the couple who are going to be its parents. In other words – this is what the images in the lower half of the purple south window show – the spirit soul descending from above in the company of guardian angels unites with the embryonic, growing body provided by the parents. The task of the first twenty years is, on the one hand, to re-accustom the spirit soul to physical conditions and, on the other, to turn the body into a useable instrument for further soul and spiritual development.

At death, the spirit soul detaches itself from the body again, going back over the whole of its life in memory – thus the description of the processes experienced in the initial period after death. The path of the spirit soul thus begins with death, represented in the image of the corpse surrounded by family shown in the purple north window. From there the path goes backwards to the old man, the mature person with partner, the youth, onwards to the infant and from there to the higher spheres of the spiritual world. On this path human beings encounter the question of their relationship to Christ and the sphere of the Father God – indicated by the crosses on Golgotha and the tablets of the law. After a period measured in many centuries, the descent to earth begins again.

The rose windows

These windows deal with the dimensions connected with the purely spiritual goals of human and cosmic evolution beyond space and time, with the question of how the human being and the world are formed, what spiritual beings the human being encounters in his innermost meditation – to give but an indication of the content of the south window. The aspects hinted at in the north window are even more mysterious, dealing with the question of how human beings experience Christ and the relationship between Christ and the two beings of Lucifer and Ahriman, already portrayed in the green window.

The sequence of nine windows, executed with the same motifs as those in the first Goetheanum, terminates in the carved group of the Representative of Humanity which was intended for the back of the stage. We will encounter this work of art in the exhibition room, as we continue our tour.

A very special phenomenon of coloured light, with its coloured shadows in complementary colours and their many different combinations, can be seen most impressively in the early afternoon during the winter when the rays of the sun also immerse the north side of the auditorium in a bright light.

Assya Turgeniev, a Russian artist who had been involved with the first Goetheanum building and then worked for decades in Dornach, ground the windows in the 1930s. The red window was not completed and installed until Whitsun 1945, 17 years after inauguration of the building, as the last of the series. The window glass, approximately 17 mm-thick sheets of stained glass, was produced by a glass manufacturer in France. The sheets were coloured by adding various metals and metal salts. The red window, for instance, was stained with small traces of gold, the green window with the addition of iron salts. The forms were ground using a grinder with a flexible shaft – rather like a water-cooled dentist's drill but larger. To avoid cracking, the work had to be undertaken under flowing water. As regards the style of execution, Rudolf Steiner had suggested to Assya Turgeniev before his death that she should use a shading technique as in sketching. A sample piece in the exhibition room depicting a section of the green south window illustrates how the work is executed.

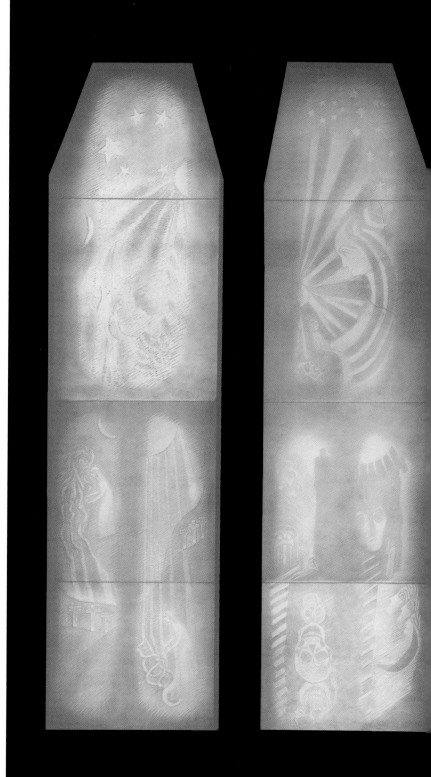

The woodwork
in the auditorium

The auditorium's acoustics

If a building is to be created as a total work of art – or at least this is to be attempted – the design issues affect every last detail: from the door handles to the shape of the green signs marking the exits, as required under building insurance regulations, and the shape of the small doors in the pillars, behind which lights belonging to the lighting system are located.

Equally the large doors to the auditorium, the organ loft and the proscenium wall are a part of the overall design, executed in elm wood rarely used today. The carving was executed by the work group mentioned above, from which the new company Baukunst also developed, supplying the blanks for the carved doors and the organ loft.

Some visitors might wonder about the significance of the high walls with a wooden rod structure at the side of the stage, above the front entrances, between the rear windows and next to the organ. These parts of the wall have been designed to absorb sound to prevent unwanted resonance. Other features in the auditorium were also introduced at the instigation of the acoustics engineer: the precisely calculated convex curve of the broad pillars next to the stage, the canopy above the proscenium, the front part of the roof shape and a number of other details. During work on the project it was fascinating to watch how each new acoustical requirement posed a new challenge for the sculptor and the architect: every such requirement had to be executed artistically and technically in such a way that an overall unity was maintained. As a result, visitors today are scarcely aware of the high degree to which art, architecture and engineering are integrated in this space.

The acoustics in the main auditorium are, in consequence, considerably better than ever before. The acoustics for music might even be described as outstanding. The finest, most subtle and barely audible tones can be heard equally in all parts of the auditorium – and large symphony orchestras or choirs can fill the auditorium with their powerful music without bludgeoning the listener. Acoustics for the spoken word, both in dramatic performances and lectures, are such that refined skills – of both delivery and attentive listening – are still required. A key factor in this respect is the level of intent with which the speaker really wishes to address the listener and the listener really wishes to understand the person speaking. That is an unfashionable requirement today. In many situations the possibility is offered, however, of using the infra red interpretation system equipment, which can offer simultaneous interpretation in five languages, as an aid to better audibility.

The organ

The organ was installed in the 1950s. A neo-romantic instrument from the Swiss organ builders Kuhn in Männedorf, the organ was completely removed and renovated as part of the redesign of the auditorium in 1996-98, reinstalled in 2000 and given a new console in 2003. The sound of the organ is traditional in character. The attempt to seek new sound characteristics and perceptions, which is an intensive preoccupation of musicians in the anthroposophical movement, was neglected here. The organ housing was carved in elm wood in 1998 in harmony with the redesign of the auditorium, as described above.

The stage

The stage curtain hides a stage of huge dimensions: 19.4 metres deep, 23 metres wide and 21.4 metres high to the fly floor; and above this a further space up to the roof. Until about 1960 this was the largest stage in Europe – so it was said – and only subsequently were larger ones built. Then there are the two side stages to the right and left in the north and south wings, where scenery and props can be prepared and moved on to the stage through wide gateways. With a proscenium structure 12 metres in height, the fly floor is roughly twice as high as the stage opening, which can vary between seven and 10.5 metres to accommodate varying production requirements. This allows scenery and curtains, veils and hanging decorations to be raised with the many different pulleys. The floor of the stage is divided into different sections which can vary in height to lower or raise the level of the stage. Various mechanical sound devices are attached to the walls – rain is produced with a pebble drum, thunder by means of steel balls falling in a wooden duct.

The basic structure of the stage equipment goes back to the early years following 1928 and has been expanded and supplemented ever since. Sadly, however, with the exception of the electrical installations, the equipment could not be totally renewed as part of the building work from 1996 to 1998. On the one hand there were insufficient resources for such a task and on the other there was no clear, commonly-agreed concept which could have been implemented with conviction and general support. This still represents a major task for the future.

However, one section of stage equipment – the lighting – has always maintained itself at the forefront of technical development over the years. Currently a wealth of more than 600 electrical circuits is utilised, with the most modern control equipment. One speciality of lighting at the Goetheanum is the endeavour to bathe the stage space in a coloured sea of light. Lighting for eurythmy does not require floodlights or targeted spotlights but generously and evenly-lit spaces. The coloured costumes of the eurythmists are immersed in various colours which can produce unexpected and subtle changes in the impression produced by the colour of a costume, depending on whether it moves in a space composed of green, blue, purple, red, yellow, white or any combination of colours. It is important in this context that this coloured space can be differentiated to the back or front, right or left, up or down. The lighting system, which includes floodlights on the floodlight bridge, on the ceiling to the left and right of the central light, and in the side pillars, is controlled from the lighting box situated on the left side under the gallery behind the last row of seats.

Goetheanum Eurythmy Ensemble

"The bride of Messina" by Friedrich Schiller

Mephisto from Goethe's "Faust"

Where can one obtain performance listings and dates for the Goetheanum stage?
Monthly programmes with previews can be picked up at the information points at any time. To register for regular mailings of the performance programme, just send a postcard requesting this. In addition, the programme of events is published regularly in the local press. All events – plays, concerts, courses, lectures, conferences, exhibitions – can be found on the www. goetheanum.org website as far in advance as they have been firmly fixed. All events are public with open access except where attendance at specialist conferences and courses requires fulfilment of specific conditions.

The realm of Ahriman
from Rudolf Steiner's
Mystery Dramas

There are some special events that particularly stand out in the history of the Goetheanum stage. The first of these was production of the four *Mystery Dramas* by Rudolf Steiner, originally staged in Munich from 1910 to 1913. From 1928 onwards they were performed on the Goetheanum stage in a new production by Marie Steiner, and in the summer of 1934 all four of them were performed in a single cycle. The second special event was the first complete performance of Goethe's *Faust*, parts I and II, in 1938. Goethe himself had the manuscript for the second part of *Faust* sealed with the condition that it only be opened after his death. Although *Faust II* was premiered in Hamburg in 1854, it remained a work which had its place in literature but not, since it was deemed impossible to perform, on the stage. Eurythmy provides so many opportunities to represent things which are thought to be beyond representation that the combination of theatre and eurythmy made the venture of an unabridged performance worth undertaking.

Since those times the *Mystery Dramas* and *Faust* have become part of the regular repertoire and are performed at the Goetheanum every three to five years.

Other classical and modern dramas, concerts and guest performances belong also to the programme.

The ground floor

The clear division of the whole building into a west and east half is also apparent on the ground floor: The east part contains all non-public rooms which belong to the stage, and the stage itself, while the west part contains spaces accessible to the public: the entrance area in the west, the information desk and ticket office, redesigned in 2006, as well as the cafeteria in the foyer. Also the cloak-room under the west staircase and the bookshop, the postcard kiosk and meeting point for guided tours, as well as the offices of two sections of the School of Spiritual Science. But the ground floor also contains the Foundation Stone auditorium, the terrace room and the English auditorium.

Foundation Stone auditorium, English auditorium and terrace room

The Foundation Stone auditorium – without a separate stage – covers exactly the same area as the stage of the main auditorium with its proscenium above it. During the planning phase it was intended as a rehearsal stage and therefore has the same dimensions as the stage. But the artists found it unpleasant to work there because of the absence of natural light and the comparatively low ceiling, and as a result it was hardly used for this purpose. In 1952 a decision was taken to upgrade the space into an auditorium with 450 seats. To this end it was necessary to install a stage in the area of the east terrace, and today this is also equipped with technical theatre facilities. During periods of economic hardship, when resources for heating the main auditorium had to be saved and visitor numbers were low, most events took place here. But today, too, more intimate theatre performances, student performances and concerts as well as many lectures, particularly in the context of conferences, are held here. The Foundation Stone auditorium was renovated and further developed in 1989-91. In 1990 Gerard Wagner (1906-1999) designed large-scale murals based on motifs in Rudolf Steiner's sketches, and also executed the murals in the English auditorium, which was reconstructed by Rex Raab (1914-2004) between 1969 and 1971. The English auditorium is used for lectures of various kinds. Its name

derives from the fact that its reconstruction was largely financed through donations from friends and members in England.

The third such space on the ground floor, the very sparsely-furnished terrace room, is used for working groups, courses and lectures. Together with the passage area to the north wing it also provides a space for temporary exhibitions, often organised by the Art Section or in connection with specialist conferences. Other temporary exhibitions, compiled from the Goetheanum art collection or from archive material, are set up in the so-called mezzanine floor between the ground floor and the auditorium.

South wing and north wing

We have already made reference to the various development phases of the south stairwell (executed in 1930, 1951, 1993 and 2005) as an example of the way in which the Goetheanum was completed in stages. If we also include the spaces which are accessed from the south stairwell – the conference room on the first floor (1981), the exhibition hall on the fifth floor (1935) and the so-called south atelier on the sixth floor (1993) – and compare them with the north stairwell (1987-1991), the north room on the fifth floor (1986) and the north atelier on the sixth floor (1987), we can experience the way in which the various generations of architects built in the spirit of their times and on the basis of their individual design skills. The endeavour was always to integrate organically with the style of the Goetheanum as a whole, while at the same time giving each particular space its own distinctive characteristics.

What they all have in common is their use of colour. Whereas in the 1950s the grey of the concrete predominated everywhere outside and inside the building, colour was slowly introduced. The colour design of the stairwells illustrates particularly well how the technique of lazure and flowing transitions from one colour to another enliven a wall, and give a sense of permeability and expansiveness, in contrast to the deadening effect from painting it in a dense, solid colour. Here, at a time when white, grey and black predominated, the courage to use colour was able to demonstrate its effect on the human being's inner life of soul. The colour designer Fritz Fuchs from Sweden (born 1937) played a key role in the colour designs executed in the 1980s.

Hidden areas

There are additional rooms, niches, corridors and staircases behind, above and below the spaces open to the public. Let us start with the hollow space around the main auditorium. There is a large space between the ceiling and the roof, extending to seven metres in some places. Mighty trusses span the whole area and bear the roof; and to these are attached steel rods which carry the ceiling. The central lighting bridge with the central light is also suspended here. At the side, this empty space passes over into the overhanging areas and free-standing pillars on the terrace which interestingly, however, do not have any structural, load-bearing functions. Stairs in the area of the terrace pillars link the highest platform with the two prop stores, created as a result of the redesign of the auditorium between the architraves and the external wall – that is, above the entrances to the seating between the pillars and the external wall. Here several thousand theatre costumes are stored as well as props ranging from elf wings to the skull which lies on the desk in Faust's study. From here one gains access to the approximately 80 cm-wide spaces between the stained-glass windows and the protective armoured glass of the external windows. From here, too, there is access to the pillars which contain the lighting gear for the stage lighting, as well as the dome over the west staircase. The achievement of the Goetheanum's designers and builders is impressively evident here.

All three sides of the stage tower contain further rooms which are partly used to store props, partly for the wardrobe and partly for offices. The floors are accessible, to staff and stage workers only, from two staircases. The north-east staircase still remains in the unfinished state of 1928 – the rough iron reinforcements of the banister still await the plasterer and, indeed, the donor who will provide the resources to finish it. The three 10 metre-high scenery stores north of the Foundation Stone stage and the main stage are connected by a powerful goods lift of the same height, which was built in the early years of the building and was renovated in 1997.

And now, down into the basement. Only a part of the Goetheanum has a basement; the rooms are mostly cramped and low. In the west section there are only connecting passages for technical conduits and wiring. In 1990 and 1997 the basement rooms under the open area to the north were significantly expanded. They now contain archives, storage rooms, large water basins and technical equipment rooms. From there, a passable underground energy supply passage connects the Goetheanum with the Heating Plant which provides the hot water for heating and ventilation.

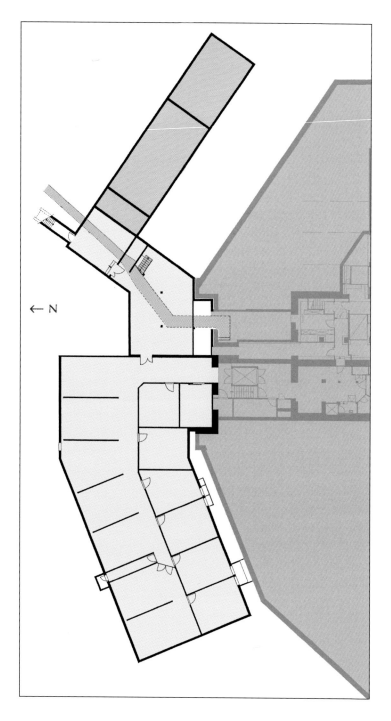

← N

Among the rooms hidden from public view, there are in fact no religious or meditation rooms, which is something people often ask about. The Goetheanum is a theatre, cultural and conference building, not a church: the anthroposophical path of schooling does not include group meditation. Meditation belongs to the area of each person's very individual schooling. That many visitors nevertheless experience a mood in many rooms which they otherwise encounter only in churches is due to the fact that they have so far only experienced a sense of spirituality in churches and not in any other context of their lives.

Blue   Water reservoirs
Yellow   Store-rooms
Orange   Underground passage
        to the heating plant
Grey   Goetheanum

Ventilation and water basins

We will briefly describe just two of the approximately 12 ventilation systems in the various areas of the building. In the basement, fresh air is drawn in from an open space between the main building and the terrace in the north east, which, once it has passed through the heating units, is driven through large-gauge ducts past the proscenium into the hollow space under the floor of the auditorium. Each seat has a round outlet. The large diameter of the ducts and the distribution of the incoming air to many openings serves the purpose, on the one hand, of creating the minimum amount of ventilation noise – the ventilation engineers were asked to meet extremely strict noise-reduction requirements for the ventilation system – and, on the other hand, of making the airflow as slow as possible to avoid the audience feeling that they are sitting in a draught.

The air which circulates through the auditorium in this way is collected again above the ceiling through openings over the glass windows and through the central light fixture, and expelled through an opening in the roof. But before the air is expelled, its heat is removed with a heat pump, taken back to the cellar and used again to heat the fresh incoming air. It is also possible to cool the air – not in the way we are accustomed from American-style air conditioning, where even you would rather put your jacket on, but in such a way that the air in the auditorium can be reduced by 7°C in relation to the outside temperature. This is done by using the two large basins of water comprising 160 m³ of rain water and 220 m³ of sprinkler water. The sprinkler water is intended, as the name suggests, for the sprinkler system as fire protection, since this requires a quantity of water within the shortest period of time that is greater than the public water supply provides. The second water basin holds rain water collected from the roofs and the terrace of the Goetheanum and is available for the fire-fighting mains system. But this water is simultaneously used at the terminal of the fire mains for flushing the toilets. Using heat pumps, the water in the sprinkler basin is cooled to approx. 6°C and the surplus heat conducted to the rain-water basin. The water cooled in this way during the night with cheap off-peak electricity is then conducted during the day through the ventilation units to cool the air in the auditorium by the 7°C mentioned earlier.

The second major ventilation system we will describe here starts by drawing in the air at the same place as the first system, but then conducting it to the cloakroom area. Part of it is taken on through the toilets and is then expelled upwards at the sides of the north and south wings, while the rest goes to the west staircase from where it rises to the space between the ceiling and the roof of the main auditorium, to be expelled through the roof of the south wing.

In all these technical systems, administrative managers at the Goetheanum building were very concerned to combine, as far as restricted financial resources allowed, modern technology, ecological perspectives and the architectural requirements of the building.

Problems of concrete

In our tour of the terrace, let us also cast our eye on concrete itself as the material from which the Goetheanum was built. We have already mentioned how the shuttering for the dynamic forms of the west porch was inspired by ship-building techniques. On flat areas of wall we can see in many places the different widths, lengths, and grains of the planking used for the shuttering. In other places, however, the surface has already weathered to such a degree that the planking texture has disappeared. In a few, particularly artistically worked places, the concrete has been bush-hammered, for example to the right and left of the west portal at terrace height around the side windows. This reveals the pebbles which are otherwise only exposed by weathering. At the same time the impression of a monolithic whole arises – ideally one could imagine the whole Goetheanum surface treated in this way.

Will the Goetheanum remain grey? Was that really the intention?
The concept of exposed concrete did not yet exist in 1928. It is not known whether Rudolf Steiner intended subsequently to plaster the concrete and possibly to paint or stain the plaster as he had done with other buildings. The files from the time merely note that "the matter still needs to be discussed". In the meantime, however, the building in its present form, that is, without plaster and paint, has acquired historical status. There are no plans to change that. On this basis the authorities decided in 1993 to make the Goetheanum a protected building under cantonal and national legislation.

A special problem is caused by concrete's so-called carbonation. This is a chemical change which affects all concrete. It spreads slowly from the outside to the inside. The result of the change is that the concrete – without affecting its hardness, static equilibrium or other cohesion – becomes permeable to water. If the process proceeds to a stage where the concrete becomes carbonised and thus permeable to water in the region of iron reinforcement at the core, the iron starts to rust. This Goetheanum concrete, mixed with quite a lot of water at the time, carbonises relatively quickly. Then there is the additional factor that the reinforcements are positioned at irregular distances

from the surface. Since rust has a greater volume than iron, it begins to expand and crack the concrete above it. This has a doubly damaging effect: on the one hand, the iron loses its structural function through rusting and no longer holds the walls together, and, on the other hand, the concrete begins to crack and crumble.

When the Goetheanum was built, such long-term effects on concrete were not yet known. Not until the 1960s did the problem become the subject of scientific research and numerous experiments. Such inspections and experiments were also carried out at the Goetheanum. First repairs of small areas were undertaken in the early 1970s, and scaffolding surrounded the whole building. The terrace followed in the 1980s, and in the 1990s it became clear that the whole building would have to be examined in the light of this problem and renovated. It was not until the period from 1993 to 1996 that the stage section, posing few problems in terms of its design, was renovated using one of the most radical methods available. About five centimetres of concrete were removed from all three walls using water at extremely high pressure, rusted iron rods were replaced with new reinforcements and a new layer of concrete, about seven centimetres thick, was cast which had to be bonded as firmly as possible with the existing concrete. Rubber moulds were produced for shuttering with the purpose of reproducing wood-shuttering patterns as accurately as possible, to match the original character of the surface structure. The concrete mixture used in this process, but above all the process used to work the concrete during application and in the days immediately following, will ensure that carbonation will now take centuries to reach the iron that is now deeply enough embedded.

But this method is not suitable for the complicated forms of the north and south wings, and above all the west section. How could shuttering identical with the present forms ever be created? For this reason further experiments have been undertaken since 1996, using new methods only developed since the last renovation. Instead of casting new concrete sections the attempt is being made to spray them. At the same time, new hydrophobic materials, i.e. colourless chemical substances, are now available for impregnating the concrete. These repel the water to stop the rusting process.

Serious action needs to be taken in coming years if the Goetheanum building is not gradually to suffer serious deterioration. At the same time it must be said, however, that the quality of the concrete work undertaken when the building was first constructed represents an extraordinary achievement, against the odds of a pioneering situation and lack of technology. The consequences of carbonation have been far less than in similar buildings from the same period. Furthermore there are no cracks in any part of the building which would raise concerns in relation to its static equilibrium.

Landscape design, the Felsli spur and the memorial grove

Let us take another walk around the terrace, this time looking at the Goetheanum's immediate surroundings. The outlook to the Felsli spur in the south-west of the building is striking. Together with the paths mentioned above, from the Speisehaus restaurant up to the Goetheanum, and the design of the space around the building to the circular area in the west with the "dragon's tail", these forms go back to the landscape design around the first Goetheanum. Rudolf Steiner devoted as much care to these features as to all other details of the building. He was liberal in his approach to the site's transformation. The material excavated for the building's foundations was not taken away to distant dumps as is the case today, but instead he boldly used it to sculpt the landscape. In this respect there is particular emphasis on the Felsli spur at the end of the elevation on which the Goetheanum is situated, before falling away into the Birs valley. It is as if existing tensions and tendencies in the landscape are enhanced, accentuating the relationship between the buildings and the wonderful landscape.

A few years after construction, grass began to grow over the landscaped steps of the Felsli, so that by the 1980s they were no longer visible; and hardly anyone knew of the historical photos. Thus it came as a great surprise when in 1991 the forms were revealed again and the public was given access. At the same time, the Felsli was protected as a monument under cantonal and national legislation, as an example of special landscape design in connection with a building that can be seen as a total work of art.

To the north-west of the Goetheanum, even before reaching the building called Rudolf Steiner House (Halde), there is a further piece of land worth noting, the memorial grove. Between several high pines a place was established where the urns of Rudolf Steiner, Marie Steiner, Christian Morgenstern and many other people belonging to the Anthroposophical Society or movement were buried. During his lifetime, Rudolf Steiner had several urns containing the ashes of deceased friends standing on the shelves of his studio. This tradition of placing urns in the studio continued after his death. The design of the exhibition room described below included a small room for urns, in which increasing numbers of urns, most of them in the shape of a pentagon dodecahedron made of copper, were deposited. In the course of the decades, this room also became too small. Cupboards and basement rooms were called into service until the management of the Goetheanum decided at the end of the 1980s to surrender the ashes from all these urns to the earth. The memorial grove was created for this purpose in 1991-93. Wive Larsson (1925-2007), a Swedish artist, designed the sculpture which now stands between the pines. The urns whose ashes were surrendered to the earth here were used to cast the bronze. Christian Hitsch and assistants designed

the stone slab, made of Brazilian granite, with its inscription and rose cross. The current design of the memorial grove was not completed until 2003.

The twelve or so hectares of land which make up the Goetheanum campus were landscaped in many different ways in the course of the decades. Starting with clear, angular forms, corresponding to the building, and with a hard surface directly surrounding the Goetheanum, the degree to which the garden is landscaped begins to lessen the further we move away from the Goetheanum, giving way to apparently uncontrolled growth. The bio-dynamically cultivated garden, border and meadow areas contain a unique wealth of indigenous plants and – particularly in the meadows to the west and south-east of the Felsli – a significant diversity of species of small fauna: grasshoppers, crickets, caterpillars and butterflies some of which are very rare. In the main part of the garden, in the upper part of the site, herbs, plants used for dyes, medicinal herbs, vegetables and flowers are grown. Efforts are made to supply the flowers for the Goetheanum from these gardens throughout the year. The vegetables are supplied to the Speisehaus restaurant or sold locally.

Whereas at the start of the twentieth century cherry trees typical of the region covered the whole of the site, a range of different fruit trees are now cultivated. Unfortunately, large numbers of conifers, which did not fit into the landscape at all, were grown for a period, partly on instruction from the authorities "to hide the view of the ugly Goetheanum" (in the north, towards Arlesheim). As late as 1995, giant Douglas firs surrounded the carpentry building. This aberration was largely rectified in recent years even if some lovers of the natural environment were violently opposed to felling trees. But the architectural forms of the Goetheanum are now permanently and irrevocably hidden from the West because the oak wood on the western slope has grown very high. This wood is now protected under woodland-preservation legislation.

The site also includes a series of sculptures which have been set up at strategic points in the landscape. The sculpture by Wive Larsson and the stone slab in the memorial grove have already been mentioned. Not far distant from it there are the figure of an angel and the sculpture "life-lines" by Gero Müller-Goldegg. The mighty "Angel of Zervreila" by Raoul Ratnowsky (1912-1999) is located in a strategic position between the carpentry building and Schuurman House. Four fine sundials on steles by Mirela Faldey, designed by Christian Hitsch, cast their spell next to the Kepler Observatory.

The buildings on the site

The carpentry building

The carpentry building was built as early as 1913 as a provisional building for the carpentry and joinery work for the first Goetheanum, a simple utilitarian, shed-like construction, erected directly on the clay without foundations except in those places where heavy machinery required them. The carpentry building today covers a relatively large area of 2800 m², now slightly more extensive than in the early years. The machine room, workshop area and storage rooms were grouped separately under three sections of roof. But soon the carpentry building acquired quite a different significance. Rudolf Steiner started to hold regular lectures for members there, and later also for the building workers. Rehearsals for the eurythmy performances also started being held there while the first building was still awaiting completion. Rudolf Steiner set up his own studio in the building which was supplemented by a second studio, the so-called sculpture atelier with an internal height of 11 metres, which was added in the spring of 1916. We will return to the role of this sculpture atelier in connection with the wooden carving depicted below.

The first Goetheanum burned down on 31 December 1922. On 1 January, at lightning speed, a free space was created between the machines and stores so that the Christmas conference, which was underway then, could continue punctually in the afternoon at five o'clock with

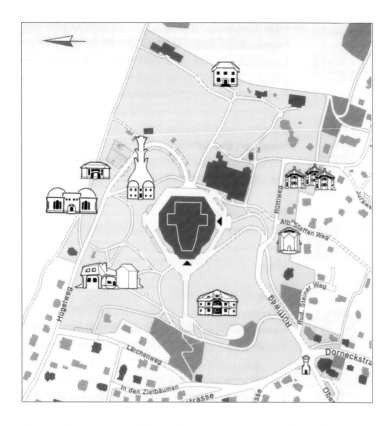

room. This is where he spent the last six months of his life and this is where he died on 30 March 1925. The way that the studio is now set out recalls the founder of anthroposophy, the architect, the artist, the scientist, the great initiate of the twentieth century.

It is one of the paradoxes of history that temporary arrangements often last longer than anything else. And yet the whole carpentry building complex has been in need of repair for years. In the 1980s the decision was taken to finish and renovate the three parts of the complex – the carpentry building auditorium, Rudolf Steiner's studio and the sculpture atelier – to preserve them for the future. That meant first laying down proper foundations under the wooden structure. Particularly in relation to the sculpture atelier, which had originally been built in the same simple barracks style, the question arose as to how the carpentry building complex should be finished. It was decided to adopt a design by Christian Hitsch, giving the sculpture atelier a form and colour which blended with the existing buildings, particularly the Goetheanum and De Jaager House nearby. The sculpture atelier was rather special in any case in the sense that the west door and the adjacent windows from the ruins of the first Goetheanum had been fitted in 1924, thus providing a living commemoration of the first building.

There is a further memorial to the fire: a pear tree stands between the carpentry building and the Goetheanum, below which is an inviting bench. Lingering there one can see what height the tree was on New Year's Eve 1922 from the height of the deep scars extending upwards on the Goetheanum side.

the performance of the *Oberufer Paradise Play*. All events took place here until the inauguration of the second building. Particularly memorable in this respect is the Christmas conference of 1923-24, at which the Anthroposophical Society was re-founded. This event took place in the hall of the carpentry building which had been extended in the preceding days by an extension to the north; at the same time the partitions to the south rooms were removed to accommodate the 800 or so participants.

The most significant of Rudolf Steiner's sculptural works was created in the studio during these years, while Edith Maryon (1872–1924), the English sculptor who assisted Rudolf Steiner in his sculptural work, worked primarily in the sculpture atelier next door. From October 1924 onwards the studio turned into Rudolf Steiner's sick

Glass House and Heating Plant

 Let us look northwards. There we can see the first two buildings – other than the provisional carpentry building – to be built on the site: the Glass House in 1914 and the Heating Plant in 1915. The Glass House was also constructed as a workshop, on the one hand for the construction office, on the other for the studio in which the glass for the auditorium was to be ground. Hence the name Glass House. The windows of the studio were given the same form and size as those of the Goetheanum.

The wooden construction of the Glass House, the cupolas and the Norwegian slate used for the roof give something of an impression of how the first Goetheanum was constructed. One also gains a clear sense that the building represents a metamorphosis of the Goetheanum, like all the other buildings designed by Rudolf Steiner for the site. As a result the so-called "auxiliary buildings" fit together in a cohesive whole.

Today the Glass House is the base of the Natural Science Section and the Section for Agriculture. The tall studios have long since been divided into several floors through the insertion of intermediate storeys to create more working space. A total restoration of the building was done in 2006. The larch shingles shine again in fresh colour. Following the restoration the Glass House, the Heating Plant and the De Jaager House were classified as monuments under cantonal and national protection.

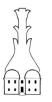 The Heating Plant was constructed in 1915 as the first concrete building on the site. It housed the coal-fired heating for the Goetheanum, connected to the latter by a passable energy duct. The tall chimney represents an impressive image of the rising flames – we can speak here of expressionist architecture. This building, too, fits into the series of metamorphoses of the buildings surrounding the Goetheanum: the two cupolas, facing the Goetheanum, are very much reduced in dimension and equal in size, whereas the centre part, which in the Glass House lies in the central area of the terrace between the two cupolas, soars up in the Heating Plant to form the chimney and the rear section with its rough cube, which anticipates the stage section in the second Goetheanum.

The Heating Plant was completely renovated in 1990 and the crumbling sections replaced using gunite. The old coal-fired heating has been replaced by a modern combination of a gas-fired block heat and power station with a gas burner which can be converted to oil as necessary. The block heat and power station produces approximately 250 kW of heat as well as 190 kW of electricity. Any surplus electricity not used by the Goetheanum is fed into the local power grid. Heat from the Heating Plant is supplied not just to the Goetheanum but also the carpentry building and a further 12 buildings distributed over the site which are connected by an extensive network of pipes.

Duldeck House

 Proceeding by historical progression, the next building is Duldeck House, built in 1915 to the west of the Goetheanum. This house's construction was "tolerated" (German: *dulden*) near the main building. Dr. Grosheintz (1867–1946), the donor of a large part of the land on which the Goetheanum was built, had his own private house built here for which Rudolf Steiner created the model. Like the Glass House and the Heating Plant, it fits completely into the language of forms of the first Goetheanum with the two powerfully implied cupolas. Here, too, concrete and brick were used as in the Heating Plant, and not wood. What might at first sight give something of a ponderous impression turns out to be alive and dynamic if one immerses oneself in the language of forms. As part of the renovation of the building in 1996, Duldeck House was the third location on the Dornach hill to be issued with a preservation order.

Today, the Trustees of Rudolf Steiner's Estate (*Nachlassverwaltung*) are located in Duldeck House; they manage Rudolf Steiner's complete literary and artistic estate in the Rudolf Steiner Archive, and publish the complete edition (*Gesamtausgabe* = GA) of his works. Since 2002, most of the archive material has been kept in a large subterranean cellar below the meadow facing the Goetheanum.

The Eurythmeum – "Rudolf Steiner House"

 "Rudolf Steiner House", simply called "Halde" in Dornach, to the north-west of the Goetheanum, is a complex which was assembled in three construction phases. The oldest section, the so-called Brodbeck House, saw the start of anthroposophical activities on the Dornach hill. Built in approximately 1905, and one of the few houses between the village centres of Arlesheim and Upper Dornach, it became the holiday and weekend home of the Grosheintz family from Basle, providing the basis for Dr. Grosheintz's offer to Rudolf Steiner to make available his land for building the Goetheanum. Rudolf Steiner stayed there in October 1912 and spring 1913 to explore the area and to see whether it was a fitting spot. Since then Brodbeck House has been the scene of numerous activities. In 1923/24 Rudolf Steiner had his own work and living rooms set up on the upper floor – but his illness prevented him ever moving in. Marie Steiner subsequently lived there for almost 20 years and this is also the place where the publication of Rudolf Steiner's works began, the work of the Trustees of Rudolf Steiner's Estate.

The next addition was the Eurythmeum in 1924, the large extension towards the north built to a model by Rudolf Steiner. The building was constructed for the arts – primarily eurythmy and theatre. The ground floor houses a large rehearsal space where Marie Steiner rehearsed the large productions of the 1920s and 1930s with actors and eurythmists. Above it was the studio where the painter Mieta Waller-Pyle (1883–1945) initially worked. Whereas all buildings planned by Rudolf Steiner are symmetrical, this is the only building to deviate from that principle since it is an extension. Rudolf Steiner ingeniously solved the problem of how a new section could be added – as a complete and independent unit, yet connected with what had been there before.

In 1935, another extension, containing a further hall, was constructed on the east side. This was executed by Albert von Baravalle in the office of Ernst Aisenpreis.

Following the move of the Trustees of Rudolf Steiner's Estate to Duldeck House, the "Halde" underwent complete and urgently necessary renovation in 2003-2004. The east extension now houses the Felicia puppet theatre; the north extension, the Eurythmeum, is still occupied by the large space for eurythmy and theatre rehearsals, and the studio above it is used for courses and conferences. The Section for the Literary Arts and Humanities, the Section for Social Sciences and a part of the Goetheanum administration are housed in Brodbeck House.

De Jaager House, Publisher's Building, Schuurman House, Eurythmy Houses

Three further buildings were created in the final years of Rudolf Steiner's work. In 1921 De Jaager House was built to the south of the Goetheanum, as a studio and residential building which the widow of the Belgian sculptor Jacques de Jaager commissioned as an exhibition and memorial space for the works of the artist and as living quarters for herself. Rudolf Steiner produced the model for it which was executed by the young architect Paul H. Bay. It is a particularly interesting fact that at a time when the first Goetheanum was still standing, a language of forms developed here which already had a tendency towards something sharp-edged and angular, anticipating the language of forms of the second Goetheanum. The basic form of the dual cupolas has been transformed here to such an extent, that the one part rises upwards as the studio space whereas the other part, comprising the residential area, is attached to it on three sides. The De Jaager House is still a residential building today, where descendants of the de Jaager family live.

The next in the sequence of buildings by Rudolf Steiner was the so-called Publisher's Building between the Heating Plant and the Glass House. It was built at a time when the first Goetheanum had already burned down and the plans for the second one did not yet exist. The Publisher's Building was built in light-weight construction within a very short period of time as a store for the books of the Philosophic-Anthroposophic Publisher's Building, which moved to Dornach from Berlin shortly

before Christmas 1923. With its immense simplicity and yet possessing tensile spatial relationships, this relatively small building is situated on the access route to the Goetheanum. Today the Publisher's Building serves as storage for the Goetheanum art collection.

 A further building with similar simplicity of form was added in 1924. This is Schuurman House on the upper edge of the site. A Dutch musician and artist couple had it built for themselves. But it was clear from the beginning that the rehearsal rooms which were being created in the building would be available for artistic activities beyond the couple's own requirements. Today Schuurman House houses the Speech and Drama School.

At the suggestion of Rudolf Steiner's collaborator Edith Maryon, the three so-called "Eurythmy Houses" were created in 1920. They were intended to provide cheap accommodation for staff at the Goetheanum, who supported the reconstruction task with great economic sacrifice and minimal incomes. Her designs for this social housing were modified and supplemented by Rudolf Steiner. Since 2007 the Karl König Archive is located in one of these houses.

And finally, mention should also be made of the electricity sub-station designed by Rudolf Steiner in 1921 near the Speisehaus restaurant. Like the Heating Plant, it gives some indication of how he saw functional buildings and how he wished to express the purpose of such buildings in their forms.

Later buildings on the site: Laboratory, Student Hostel, Kepler Observatory, Wooden House

No more building took place on the site until the 1960s. The architect Alexander Tschakalow (1909–1992) built the Crystal Laboratory in 1960 and a little later the Kepler Observatory as a building for the Section for Mathematics and Astronomy. The observatory with its outstanding telescope is often open for visitors late into the night and the phenomena of the night sky can be admired with a knowledgeable guide. The Student Hostel with space for about 35 students of the various seminars in Dornach was created in 1969-70, designed by the architect Fritz Müller from Öhringen, Stuttgart.

For various reasons no other building was built on the site apart from an electricity sub-station largely covered in earth and designed by Rex Raab. The 1992 zoning plan prohibited further building on a considerable part of the site, and the costs of necessary and unavoidable restoration and renovation, some of it very urgent, were so great that no financial resources were left over for new projects.

It is clear that Rudolf Steiner wished to construct a whole range of further buildings on the site. A clinic was planned for the south-east corner. This never came about. In the years from 1927 to 1931 the only building to be built on the Goetheanum site was Pyle House, which however always remained in private ownership.

A topographical model is kept in the Goetheanum of the immediate surroundings with all the buildings. The buildings designed by Rudolf Steiner himself are marked in a violet-blue colour.

The "Colony"

From the very beginnings of building activity at the Goetheanum, that is, from as early as 1913, Rudolf Steiner was concerned to ensure that the residential properties subsequently built by anthroposophists in the vicinity of the Goetheanum should fit into the whole in terms of their style, thus implementing the architectural idea of organic building. With the examples of Duldeck House and De Jaager House he himself demonstrated how much the external forms of such buildings could be transformed and yet fit into the whole. Since then much has been created over the decades which gives the "Colony" or the "Hill", as it is referred to in the village, its special characteristics. Generations of architects have attempted to find their own style, based on a thorough study and investigation of the building forms of the first and second Goetheanums.

There is only space here to show photos of a few of the approximately 100 buildings which were designed on this basis in Dornach and Arlesheim. New ones continue to be added almost every year.

Julian House, built 1987, architect Conrad Hoenes
Siebeneck House, built 1915, architect unknown
Achteck House, built 2000, architect Ulrich Oelssner
Hofmann House, built 1956, architect Albert von Baravalle, now house of the Medical Section at the Goetheanum

The first Goetheanum

Rust House, built 1934, architect Erwin Drescher
Jung House, built 1957, architect Alexander Tschakalow

Early history

Anthroposophical activities started in 1902 in connection with the then Theosophical Society in Berlin, whose general secretary Rudolf Steiner had become. In what started out as small groups, work was undertaken on many subjects. The groups became larger and new groups started in other German cities, Austria and Switzerland. The European Section of the Theosophical Society held annual congresses. In 1907 the German section under the leadership of Rudolf Steiner issued invitations to a congress in Munich. Here it became evident for the first time that the subjects at issue were not just philosophical in nature and about our view of the world, but that an artistic impulse was also seeking new forms of expression, in relation to interior decoration of the rooms. Rudolf Steiner designed panels for the congress hall which for the first time showed the motifs later developed in the pillars with their capitals, and large picture panels with the designs for the seals of the Apocalypse. The planetary seals appeared on the programme, the room was draped in a deep red material, and busts of Fichte, Schelling and Hegel stood on the stage. But the emphasis was not just on the visual arts. A group of actors performed the mystery play *The holy drama of Eleusis* by the French esotericist and poet Edouard Schuré.

> *For as long as we are forced to meet in such venues, whose forms belong to a declining culture, our work must, to a greater or lesser extent, be affected by the destiny of what is in decline. The spiritual stream will only be able to introduce the new culture, as is its task, when granted the opportunity to work right down into the physical design, the very walls of the buildings which surround us. And spiritual life will have a quite different effect when it flows from spaces whose dimensions are determined by the science of the spirit, whose forms have been created on the basis of spiritual science.*
>
> Rudolf Steiner, 3.1.1911, GA 284

All of this was alien to many of the then members of the Theosophical Society and, together with differences of opinion about content, laid the foundations for the separation of the anthroposophical movement from the Theosophical Society. The split which finally took place in late 1912 was the result, not least, of Rudolf Steiner's wish to pursue a European Christian path which was clearly different from the eastern path pursued by theosophy.

Holding a summer congress in Munich became something of a tradition in the following years. In 1910 this led to the premier of Rudolf Steiner's first mystery drama, which in grand images presents the inner drama of the reciprocal relationships between a group of people, delving deep into the background of connections and relationships of destiny among them as far back as previous earth lives. In the following years until the outbreak of the First World War three further mystery dramas by Rudolf Steiner were performed.

All these events took place in rented theatres or congress halls. This led to the wish for the movement to have its own building in which, on the one hand, anthroposophical work could take place throughout the year and where, on the other, the artistic work and meetings could take place in a space whose outer forms and colours also corresponded to the spirit of anthroposophical activity.

The architect Schmid-Curtius was commissioned to draw up plans for a property in Munich. The initiative had come from the group of people around Rudolf Steiner and Steiner himself had made key suggestions: it was to be a building with dual cupolas whose two differently sized spheres were to intersect in a specific relationship. But the plan encountered resistance from the city authorities, the adjacent church and local neighbours. The negotiations dragged on and it was not at all certain whether anything would ever come of it. Rudolf Steiner, who saw the First World War looming, pushed very hard to realise the building.

Dr. Grosheintz from Basle, a dentist who felt a very close connection to the movement, knew about these difficulties. When Rudolf Steiner came to Basle in the autumn of 1912 to deliver his lecture cycle on the Gospel of St Matthew, Grosheintz invited him to come to House Brodbeck – as mentioned above. Rudolf Steiner asked him what he intended to do with the land. As a consequence, Grosheintz made it available for the building. Rudolf Steiner returned in March 1913 and together with the architect he surveyed the land in extensive walks through the property and the wider surroundings as far as the hermitage at Arlesheim.

Apart from the hermitage, there were also other interesting locations in the immediate surroundings. It is said, after all, that there were holy sites here even in pre-Christian times. At a later time, events connected with Parsifal took place in the area. The mound on which the Goetheanum is situated belongs to the battlefield of the battle of Dornach on 22 July 1499 in which Switzerland definitively extricated itself from the Holy Roman Empire. The part of

the mound east of the Goetheanum is still referred to as the "blood mound" today, and the Hügelweg path was called "blood mound path" until the 1930s. Arlesheim nearby is a further location where the Bishop of Basle took up residence after he had been driven out of the city as part of the Reformation. And Basle itself is close by – an ancient cultural centre with an openness for future-orientated impulses.

Schmid-Curtius began to rework the plans intended for Munich. This was necessary because in Munich the building would have been situated between other large buildings whereas here it was to stand alone on a hill, freely visible from all sides. In the following months,

Rudolf Steiner made parts of an exterior model with the terrace and side wings on a scale of 1:20 which today are exhibited in the exhibition room.

The decision to build in Dornach was not taken until June 1913, but then everything moved very fast. The foundation stone was laid as early as 20 September 1913. Work proceeded intensively over the winter. Up to 600 building workers were present on the building site at the same time and the topping-out ceremony was celebrated on 1 April 1914. Workers in the building trades, above all carpenters, had come from all over Central Europe, and wood merchants even say that the price of wood rose because of the large quantities required for the Goetheanum.

Managing the building site with so many workers was a huge challenge. For a short period double shifts were tried, with the Birseckbahn tram extending its timetable in the morning and evening to cope with the extra demand. But a meeting of building workers at the end of the working week, that is, at 5 p.m. on a Saturday, demanded that shift work be discontinued.

The situation became much more difficult with the outbreak of the First World War in the first days of August 1914. Many of the artists who had come to work on carving the capitals and architraves had to leave, only to end up fighting against one another in the various European armies. Work slowed down a great deal, the financial funding no longer flowed to the same extent. And yet in the midst of a warring Europe people from 16 different nations worked peacefully together without interruption on this common task while the sound of cannon fire could be heard from nearby Alsace. But the work took much longer than it would otherwise have done. At the same time the spiritual situation in Europe changed to such an extent, particularly towards the end of the war from 1917 onwards, that nothing seemed quite the same as before as far as social and political structures were concerned. The radical changes which had begun in art in the years before the war now also affected other areas of life.

In this situation the building, still not quite finished, did not start being used until October 1920, when a week-long course was held there.

The building

In all earlier cultures, buildings intended to nurture the soul and spiritual life of communities of people were created on the basis of spiritual impulses. The Egyptian temples and pyramids bear impressive witness to a culture characterised and led by esoteric mystery centres. In Greece the gods were present in the temples; and the devotional community, lifting its eyes to God, lived in Gothic churches. And today?

The soul and spiritual situation of modern human beings since the start of the twentieth century is characterised by a complete emancipation, developing over centuries, from the guidance of any kind of higher spiritual beings – be it in a human or divine hierarchy. Human beings have become self-reliant and look outward with their senses and intellect into the world accessible through sense perception. Such emancipation also meant that they descended deeply into materialism, particularly in the nineteenth century, to such an extent that they tried to convince themselves that there was no spiritual world lying beyond the sensory one. But with the start of the twentieth century it became evident in a variety of cultural phenomena that the yearning of people for the spirit could not be suppressed and always sought new ways to come to expression. Anthroposophy is one of those ways to find renewed access to this higher world, and to pursue what it means for each person to include the spiritual dimension; and how a possible science of the spirit can influence practical spheres of life such as medicine, education, agriculture, the arts, etc.

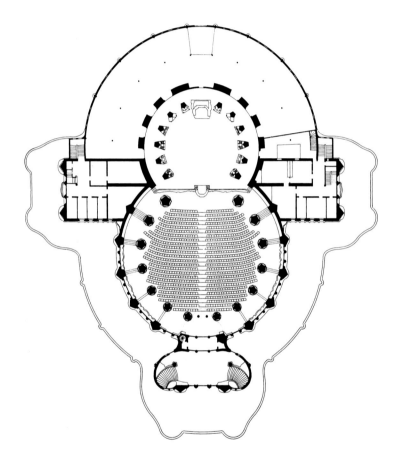

Architecture is an expression of this. Corresponding to a quite particular attitude of soul, round buildings produced in human beings a feeling of the divine which lived all around in nature, in human beings and animals, in plants and rocks. Later, corresponding to the view of a God who lives purely in the spirit and towards whom a person strives, spaces clearly directed forwards and upwards in the form of longitudinal church buildings formed the basis of the church architecture of western and central Europe.

The building constructed in the years from 1913 to 1920 must be seen in the context of the end of the Art Nouveau period, which in its own way assimilated organic elements. But what was there to follow Art Nouveau? Could an architecture develop which took the living, organic element one step further, or must architecture be reduced to functionalism and geometry, as typified by late Bauhaus?

In the first Goetheanum, Rudolf Steiner created a new type of building with dual cupolas in which the round and longitudinal aspects of the building were combined in a delicate balance. In the auditorium, people had the experience of a circular building as long as the curtain was closed and attention was not directed towards events on

the stage. As soon as the higher dimension of events on stage opened up, they had the experience of a longitudinal building.

But even in the round building under the great cupola, the forward-facing direction becomes clearly evident: seven great and strictly symmetrical pillars arise on right and left, each one slightly higher than the previous one because the floor of the auditorium slopes downwards towards the stage, rising by one step towards the back of the auditorium for each row of seats. The capitals and plinths as well as the wide-swung architrave above are images of cosmic evolution, as described above in relation to the present main auditorium. The first building did not have pillars which appear to be growing out of the wall, however, but free-standing pillars whose capitals and plinths had designs around their whole circumference. A different type of wood was used for each pillar and the architrave above it: white beech, ash, cherry, oak, elm, maple and birch. The stained-glass windows which, as we have already mentioned, were ground in the Glass House, stood illuminated between the pillars.

The large cupola vaulted above the whole space which, as in the present main auditorium, was decorated using plant colours, on the basis of Rudolf Steiner's sketches. In comparison to the present auditorium, the earlier one had a much stronger upward orientation. The arch over the proscenium was 18 m high (present stage opening 12 m), and the highest point of the cupola was 27.2 m above the ground (today 20 m).

When the curtain opened, the audience saw a fully architecturally-formed stage space. We do not really know how Rudolf Steiner intended to use it as a theatre in combination with lighting, curtains, decorations and scenery. But before the fire struck, tests with lighting for eurythmy performances had already taken place.

Twelve pillars of equal height, arranged in six symmetrical pairs, with a slightly larger gap in the middle, supported the smaller cupola. Christ and the striving human being as represented by Faust were the motifs in the cupola painting, which Rudolf Steiner undertook himself. The pillar plinths were extended to make thrones, like mighty seats. It is possible the space under the small cupola would in future have also been used for special meetings.

The large lectern, which could be lowered into the floor, was positioned at the intersection of the two spheres in front of the stage curtain; it was sculpted in the form of an artistically metamorphosed larynx. The lectern fell victim to the flames in 1922 like everything else, but a copy was made for the second Goetheanum. It thus forms the only part of the main auditorium which is an exact replica of the first building.

The gap at the centre of the series of pillars on the stage, referred to above, was intended for a huge, 9.5 m-high wooden carving. Rudolf Steiner had been working on it since 1915 with the English artist Edith Maryon. But since the carving had not been completed at the time of the fire and still stood in the studio, it survived the fire and is today located in the exhibition room. More of that below.

Further rooms were grouped around the auditorium and stage. Wardrobes and storage rooms for sets surrounded the stage, the ground floor contained the entrance hall, cloakroom and service rooms, and the two side wings held one auditorium each. The white room under the roof has become famous because the Christian Community was founded there in October 1922 and the fire was first noticed there on New Year's Eve 1922.

The cupolas were designed as a dual-layer construction with the two inner cupolas resting on the pillars of the auditorium and the stage, and the outer cupolas, covered in Norwegian slate, on the external walls. The distance between the two sets of cupolas was about three metres. The large and small inner and outer cupolas were not structurally dependent on one another, each dome being designed to support itself. It was an exciting moment when the construction supports were removed from underneath the cupolas and everyone waited to see how both cupolas would behave: after a brief oscillation, they remained in their calculated positions.

Old maps still designate the building as "Johannes-Bau", named after one of the central figures in Rudolf Steiner's mystery dramas, Johannes Thomasius. The name "Goetheanum" was not commonly used until about 1918.

> *Why is the building called after Goethe? What is the connection between anthroposophists and Goethe?* Even as a young man, Rudolf Steiner was closely involved with Goethe's works when a science student of physics, chemistry and mathematics. At the age of only 21 he was asked to participate in editing the Weimar edition of Goethe's works and was subsequently given responsibility for editing Goethe's scientific writings. Rudolf Steiner discovered the basis for his own way of thinking and epistemology in Goethe's scientific method. But the literary writings of Goethe – who was deeply familiar with esoteric perspectives and presented a number of these aspects in his literature, even if sometimes in a very veiled way – also provided a starting point for Rudolf Steiner's epistemological endeavours to establish a modern science of the spirit. In view of these links to Goethe, and in homage to this greatest genius in the German history of ideas, the name "Goetheanum" was chosen.

In Rudolf Steiner's time, the building stood widely visible on the hill, not surrounded by the many buildings there are today. It must have produced a tremendous impact on his contemporaries. The extraordinary nature of the building was discussed in newspaper articles in many countries. At the same time the building illustrated that these rather unusual anthroposophists had to be something more than some small insignificant group if they were capable of managing such a large-scale construction project. But the other side of that coin was that it also initiated the hostility towards the anthroposophists and

their building which was discussed in the chapter on the history of the second building. This often took an openly libellous form, and a catholic priest in Arlesheim was particularly vociferous in this respect. But in Germany, too, the hostility and thuggish behaviour towards Rudolf Steiner went so far that massive disruptions of his public lectures forced the cancellation of a lecture tour. From this time onwards he only held his lectures among groups of members in Germany, whereas in Switzerland public lectures were still possible even after these events.

It remains an open question as to whether this climate of hostility or other reasons led to the disaster which followed: the fire which was started on New Year's Eve 1922. The fire must have been started in the course of the afternoon: it was done very cleverly, as a smouldering fire between the walls which spread slowly but surely without being noticed. It flared up once visitors had left the building after the evening lecture. It did not take long for the building to go up in flames and at midnight, while the church bells were ringing in the New Year in surrounding villages, the main cupola collapsed and the flames turned to lurid colours as the metal organ pipes also started to burn. All that remained was a ruin which continued to smoulder for days afterwards.

The fire did not achieve its purpose of delivering a fatal blow to the anthroposophical movement. Life continued without interruption, as described in the first chapter on the history of the movement. But this instantaneous destruction of work which had required many years of sacrifice produced a deep caesura in the life of many people who had worked on the building, and in particular Rudolf Steiner. Edith Maryon, Rudolf Steiner's artistic collaborator, became seriously ill and never recovered; Rudolf Steiner's health also suffered to such an extent that – compounded by other factors – his strength was sapped. Then there was the issue of the huge financial resources which had been spent on the building. The Solothurn Building Insurance company had to cope with a claim of unprecedented proportions which threw it into severe difficulties. The insured sum of 1.5 million Swiss francs at the then value provided the basis for re-building. But Rudolf Steiner had major reservations about using this money since it did not derive from the sacrifice of willing donors – as was really necessary from a spiritual perspective for a building of this nature – but was provided reluctantly by each insurance policy holder in the canton in accordance with statutory regulations.

The building as an archetypal image of a modern mystery centre building remained deeply embedded in the memory of those who witnessed it. Many of them measured everything that followed against this image for the rest of their lives. And subsequent generations of anthroposophists, particularly architects, sculptors and painters, never stopped studying the forms and colours of the building. As set out in the section on "The building as an expression of anthroposophy", this is not restricted to artistic aspects of the building but concerns an inner understanding of what took visible shape at the time, and what anthroposophy, by this means, represented in terms that extended beyond conceptual ideas.

For some years now, the labour of a retired member of the Goetheanum staff has provided the opportunity to gain a living impression of the first Goetheanum. Since 1994, Rudolf Feuerstack has been working on a 1:20 scale model of the building which shows both the outer form and the interior of the auditorium in precise detail. It has been built on a stand which allows the observer to put his head into the auditorium from below, giving the view of someone sitting in the middle rows of the seating. The model, which is still incomplete, can be viewed as from autumn 2010 in the exhibit room.

A model of the exterior made by the architect Albert von Baravalle on a scale of 1:100 is situated in the exhibit room on the fifth floor of the south stair. Its small size should not lead us to think that the first building's dimensions were not almost as large as the second Goetheanum: height 34.3 m, length 82.5 m, width 74.3 m. The diagrams of the seals for Rudolf Steiner's four Mystery Dramas, whose performances the building was intended to house, are shown on the walls of the stair in scraped rendering.

The Representative of Humanity

Fate had clearly decreed that a part of the total work of art that was the first Goetheanum should be preserved. It had not been completed at the time of the fire, as already described, and was therefore still standing in the studio: the sculpture, carved in wood, of the "Representative of Humanity". During the night of the fire, concerned friends had carried it into the field behind the carpentry building in sections since this building, too, was threatened by the fire. But where should it be housed after the fire? Another point we have already mentioned is that the stage in the second building was to be equipped as a technical stage, and in order to realise this concept a separate exhibition space was created for the Group despite the original intention for its location. Not just the wooden carving but other objects were also to be exhibited in that room. While the second Goetheanum was still being constructed, the carving was transported in the summer of 1927 on a ramp from the carpentry building into the main building through an opening specifically for this purpose and installed inside. The space itself, as seen today, was only realised in 1935 from plans by Mieta Waller-Pyle. Sculpted plaster was used for the first time in the design of the walls, a principle which was then used 60 years later in a more advanced form in the sculpted shotcrete for the main auditorium.

Will the technical stage remain as it is now or is consideration being given to returning to the architectural design of the stage as it was in the first Goetheanum? The question as to whether the sculpture should be placed on the stage after all, making it necessary to use an architectural rather than a technical approach, has never been finally answered. The issue was debated and thought about particularly intensively during redesign of the auditorium in the 1990s. The subject is not currently under discussion.

What, then, does the carving depict? We should, here again, refrain from seeking symbolic or allegorical meanings: the carving embodies the endeavour to show a human being who represents the highest goals of human evolution. Rudolf Steiner described the main figure in the group as the "Representative of Humanity". He frequently mentioned, as well, that it was at the same time a representation of Christ.

The composition of the carving is the direct continuation and conclusion of what is depicted in the nine glass windows. This path leads to the Representative of Humanity. And just as Christ after the baptism had to deal with the devil and Satan in the desert, so the Representative of Humanity is represented here in confrontation with Lucifer and Ahriman. Lucifer as the tempter wants to lure human beings away from the earth, wants to turn them into beings who dissolve in spiritual bliss, who seek Nirvana and ignore the hardships of the world. At the same time he inspires independent thinking and art. But he bears the danger of pride and severance of the ties which bind us to our fellow human beings and the surrounding world. Lucifer is shown twice in the wooden carving, once to the left of Christ, at the same height, and once to the upper outside right at the moment when he tumbles downwards. Lucifer falls into the depths in the face of the overwhelming spiritual power of Christ.

The second figure, Ahriman, is also represented twice. Once to the left at the level of the right hand of the large human figure, and again in the depths of the earth into which he has banished himself. What forces work through Ahriman? They lead human beings to unite themselves with the material world which they need to do if they are to incarnate in a physical body. But Ahriman tries to inspire human beings to incarnate so deeply in matter that they forget their divine origin and are completely taken up with the material world and materialism. Hence the question arises how human beings can find the balance between these two forces. We should neither remain in aesthetically high-flown regions, failing to make the connection to the physical world, a connection we need in order to develop as individual people; nor must we be totally taken in by the material world and thus lose our connection to the spirit.

The composition of the carving encourages us to engage inwardly with these two ways in which we can deviate from a healthy path of development after we have progressed through the images of the nine stained-glass windows. There is still one further figure with a winged head which watches events from on high with a certain distance and a smile on its lips – like a being from spheres which are not part of this world. This figure is often described as "cosmic humour".

Head of Christ, Study to the Representative of Humanity by Rudolf Steiner

What is the "meaning" of the way the fingers are held in the large figure? Why this unusual bearing?

Before proceeding any further, it should be pointed out once more that symbolic or allegorical meanings play no part here. Rudolf Steiner and Edith Maryon endeavoured in every detail to use purely artistic methods in their representation. We experience in the slight bend of the fingers that the hand is neither bunched in a fist nor is it an expansive outward gesture. As a result, the hands are neither tense nor streaming outwards but contained. The division of the fingers into three elements comprising the thumb, index and middle finger and ring and little finger can often be found in many representations in art.

The composition of the Representative of Humanity is essentially the result of the collaboration between Edith Maryon (1872-1924) and Rudolf Steiner. The models in the so-called sculpture atelier impressively illustrate the artistic process. The first, second, fourth and fifth model are on exhibition there; the sixth, two-metre high model, executed in white plaster, is positioned in a corner of the exhibit room. But there also followed a seventh model on a scale of 1:1, which was made in the sculpture atelier specifically built for this purpose from wood, plaster, plasticine and mortar in the years from 1916 to 1917. The model was never intended to be preserved. Rudolf Steiner instructed that the parts of the seventh model which had been completed in the final carving should be destroyed. This is what happened with the main figure and Ahriman in the bowels of the earth. But by the time that Rudolf Steiner had been forced to take to his sickbed in the neighbouring studio and, all the more so after his death, no one dared to destroy what remained of the 1:1 model. Together with the preservation of what was meant to be a temporary carpentry building, it is one of the paradoxes of history that this model, which was never intended for posterity, is still in existence. The crumbling material was comprehensively restored in the 1960s, and in 1993 the building itself was renovated with cladding for the existing walls and a second roof over the original one.

It is of immense value for sculptors to be able to study the forms of the model, some of which have been completed to a much more differentiated degree than in the incomplete "original". Having been kept under lock and key for decades, unknown even to long-serving staff at the Goetheanum, the room with the model is today a study space for visual artists. The model room can be viewed by arrangement.

The models

Further important models are on show in the exhibition room e.g. an exterior model of the first Goetheanum. The copy of the paintings in the cupolas, produced in the 1930s by Hilde Boos-Hamburger who herself had been involved in the painting of the work, gives an impression of what the interior would have looked like. The interior model of the first Goetheanum, completed by Rudolf Steiner in January 1914, which was used for the actual building. The cupolas do not yet contain any designs for the painted motifs but the specified colours already provide some indication as to the planned colour dynamics. This model is now in an air conditioned room in the basement.

In addition, there is a copy of the exterior model of the second Goetheanum by Rudolf Steiner which was created in March 1924 and formed the basis for the building permit application. The copy of the model was made at a time when the original model had already sagged a little but still largely retained its original form. One can clearly see how Rudolf Steiner only developed detailed forms on the north side, which were then realised, whereas on the south side much remained only as an indication. The terrace is missing from the model since at that point Rudolf Steiner still assumed that the terrace of the first building could be saved. He never made a model for the new terrace and his suggestions are contained in just a few sketches.

Finally, the two samples of glass windows in the exhibition room should still be mentioned which show

the style and the technique which was used for processing the glass. The fragment of green glass, using the technique for today's windows, has already been mentioned in connection with the auditorium. But there is also a large fragment of glass from the first building which clearly broke during building work and which indicates the grinding techniques used at the time. The broken pane had been completely forgotten and was only rediscovered behind a cupboard in the carpentry building about 25 years ago. The surprising thing is that in 2001, in the loft of an old building near Lake Constance, a further fragment from the same pane was found and recognised as belonging to that piece of glass from the Goetheanum.

Only a small part of the art collection at the Goetheanum can be put on display in the exhibition room. The collection comprises models, drawings and watercolours by Rudolf Steiner as well as works by visual artists connected with Rudolf Steiner, and anthroposophically-inspired art from subsequent decades. There is enough material to fill several museum exhibition rooms with significant and interesting works. There have been proposals, but not as yet any concrete plans, to create an exhibition space in the area of the carpentry building.

Documentation at the Goetheanum: Art Collection, Archive and Library

With access via the east entrance of the building, the Goetheanum additionally provides a large anthroposophical public library which holds more than 100,000 titles and probably comprises all publications which have appeared in connection with anthroposophy in the last century. Linked to it are the Archive, the Art Collection and the Plan Archive of the building administrators at the Goetheanum, in which close to four million documents, many works of art and more than 8,000 architectural plans – including the plans for the first Goetheanum – have been collected, examined and ordered. There are thus still plenty of opportunities for further research. The Art Collection, Archive and Library are today combined in the "Documentation at the Goetheanum" department.

The Rudolf Steiner Archive

A second archive, the Rudolf Steiner Archive, is located in Duldeck House, as already mentioned, and is managed by the Rudolf Steiner Nachlassverwaltung, the trustees of Rudolf Steiner's estate. It contains Rudolf Steiner's estate with all his notebooks, the shorthand notes from his lectures with the blackboard drawings as well as innumerable letters. The work of this archive is devoted to publishing the complete edition of Rudolf Steiner's works, which currently comprises some 350 volumes.

Who was Rudolf Steiner?

Rudolf Steiner, born on 27 February 1861 in the border area where Austria, Croatia and Hungary meet, studied science (mathematics, physics, chemistry) in Vienna and edited Goethe's scientific writings in Weimar. Building on Goethe's epistemology, which led the latter to discover the archetypal plant and develop his theory of metamorphosis, Rudolf Steiner developed these insights further to encompass research into worlds of soul and spirit. The subsequent building in Dornach was called the Goetheanum for this reason. He presented the results of his research in writings and lectures.

Rudolf Steiner's anthroposophical activities began in Berlin in 1902. In a first phase of development, initially within the Theosophical Society of the time, he worked on philosophical issues and questions related to our understanding of the world; in a second phase, from 1907 onwards, he concerned himself intensively with the arts. The festivals in Munich with the performances of Rudolf Steiner's Mystery Dramas produced the impulse to create a building devoted to anthroposophy, the Goetheanum. A third phase of his work added the practical application of anthroposophy in many fields: medicine and pharmacy, education and special needs education, agriculture, social issues, the arts, to mention but a few. In 1923 the anthroposophical activities of the time were re-established and combined in the Anthroposophical Society. Rudolf Steiner died in Dornach on 30 March 1925.

General information, addresses

Status: Spring 2010, subject to change

Goetheanum
Rüttiweg 45, 4143 Dornach, Switzerland
Information, phone +41 61 706 42 42
Tickets and guided tours, phone +41 61 706 44 44
tickets@goetheanum.org
Further information in detail see www.goetheanum.org

General Anthroposophical Society
Allgemeine Anthroposophische Gesellschaft
    Postfach
    CH - 4143 Dornach 1
    Tel. + 41 61 706 42 72
    Fax + 41 61 706 43 14
    sekretariat@goetheanum.ch
    www.goetheanum.org.

Suggested further reading

Rudolf Steiner:
The Philosophy of Freedom. The Basis for a Modern
    World Conception, Rudolf Steiner Press, Sussex 1999.
Theosophy. An introduction to the supersensible knowl-
    edge of the world and the destination of man,
    Rudolf Steiner Press, Sussex 2005.
Occult science – an Outline, Rudolf Steiner Press,
    Sussex 2005.
Towards Social Renewal, Rudolf Steiner Press,
    London 1999.
Architecture as a Synthesis of the Arts, Rudolf Steiner
    Press, London 1999.
Architecture. An Introductory Reader, Rudolf Steiner
    Press, Sussex 2003.

For further books and lectures see the catalogues of, for
    example, Rudolf Steiner Press or SteinerBooks
    (Anthroposophic Press).

Other authors:
Kenneth Bayes, Living Architecture, Floris Books,
    Edinburgh 1994.
Werner Blaser, Nature in Building – Rudolf Steiner in
    Dornach 1913-25, Birkhäuser 2002.
Hilde Raske, The Language of Colour in the First
    Goetheanum – A Study of Rudolf Steiner's Art,
    Walter Keller Verlag, Dornach 1983.
Judith von Halle/John Wilkes, The Representative of
    Humanity, Between Lucifer and Ahriman, Rudolf
    Steiner Press, Sussex 2010.

List of illustrations